Renaissance Recipes

A detail from The Kitchen, *by Vicenzo Campi (1536-91) in the*
Pinacoteca de Brera, Milan.

Painters & Food

RENAISSANCE RECIPES

BY

GILLIAN RILEY

Pomegranate Artbooks
SAN FRANCISCO

First published 1993 by Pomegranate Artbooks
Box 6099, Rohnert Park, California 94927

Conceived, designed, and produced by
New England Editions Limited
25 Oakford Road
London, NW5 1AJ, England

ISBN 1-56640-577-7
Library of Congress Catalog Card Number 93-84099

Editor/Art Director: TRELD PELKEY BICKNELL

Book Design: GILLIAN RILEY

Jacket/cover Design: GLYNN PICKERILL

Typeset in Palatino by CHAMBERS WALLACE

Printed in Singapore by IMAGO PUBLISHING

CONTENTS

Introduction

"Trout from the Aniene", it said on the menu of the restaurant near the Temple of Vesta in Tivoli, where I had a light meal during an expedition to admire the inscription on the temple. Trout it was—and delicious; from the Aniene it was not! The Aniene is now so polluted that you would not want to wash your car in it. Six hundred years ago, Poggio Bracciolini—fired with a similar passion for ruins, but under a clearer sky—would have dined as simply and with as much pleasure, as he took a break from examining ivy-covered columns and broken arches.

The inscriptions on the Temple of Vesta have been an inspiration to architects and designers through the ages, from Alberti to Sir John Soane and Eric Gill. Indeed, a passion for the calligraphy and lettering of the past seems to inspire generations of enthusiasts to undertake endless journeys of exploration—like Mantegna and his unruly companions on the shores of Lake Garda.

At what point inscription-hunting became relegated to the short periods between meals, I shall never know; but there came a time when I found myself investigating the history of Italian food with the same devotion that Poggio applied to his predatory pursuit of classical literature and lettering. The glories of Renaissance Italy's gastronomy—discovered in libraries, restaurants, and in the kitchens of friends—turned out to be as superlative as its artistic heritage.

The period of enthusiasm for the culture of ancient Greece and Rome, which began in mid-fourteenth-century Florence, extended into the second half of the sixteenth century and stimulated a wave of creativity in all the arts. It felt like a rebirth at the time and so it has come to be called the Renaissance. Styles of painting which developed then have precise art-historical definitions, but there was a continuity in ways of cooking which happily transcends these boundaries. We unashamedly use illustrations from work outside these precise limits to accompany our selection of recipes.

From their enthusiasm for recording the art and science of the Ancient World, Renaissance thinkers went on to creative achievements of their own. The same need to discover, analyze, and codify must have motivated the compilers of the earliest-known cookery manuscripts.

Historians used to assume that cooks, like storytellers, passed on much of their skill by example and word of mouth. Probably illiterate, most cooks would have served an apprenticeship, learning their trade, as it were, on the shop floor, without the need of books. Such practical manuals as there were, would have tended to get used-to-death and then thrown away. Nevertheless, the surprisingly large number of cookery manuscripts that *have* survived are perhaps only a fraction of those in use in Renaissance Italy.

Moreover, recent research into levels of literacy in the early Renaissance indicates that many more people knew how to read and write than one might suppose. Francesco Datini's wife, Margarita, learned to write quite late in life and proceeded to make the most of her ability—by nagging him on paper as well as in person.

The cookery texts available for study were written by intelligent, well-organized, and literate people—qualities needed to run the complicated kitchens and store-rooms of a noble or papal household. Bartolomeo Scappi came from a distinguished Bolognese family. Platina, although of humble birth, was one of the foremost intellectuals of his time. Martino, whose recipes Platina used, was designated simply "Cuoco" on the title page of one version of his manuscript. But the affectionate reference to him at the end of Platina's recipe for *biancomangiare* gives hints of a strong and commanding personality: "Immortal Gods! Was there ever such a cook as my Martino? Such eloquence! You should hear him laying down the law in our Roman taverns, those grammar schools of gastronomy.... Now that's something we really can do better than the Greeks and Romans..."

Charismatic personalities leap out at one from every direction in the quest for Renaissance food: Michelangelo, apoplectic with fury at some sub-standard Trebbiano wine, or quietly content with a present of Marzolino cheeses and chick peas; the usually tactful Castelvetro berating the English over their heavy indulgence in meat; the ageing Poggio Bracciolini singing the praises of his young wife; Scappi, the master cook preparing papal banquets with hundreds of dishes; Maria Vittoria, the cheerful nun with a passion for fine food; and the bigoted, intolerant Pope Paul II, exhausted after a hard day persecuting dissidents, who ate one too many slices of iced melon on a hot summer's night in 1471 and expired of apoplexy.

———————————— ✂☙◉☙✂ ————————————

Changes in taste and style and the use of unusual ingredients make Renaissance cuisine seem at first sight rather different from modern Italian food, but delving into the traditions of regional cooking, deciphering and devouring hundreds of recipes, searching for particular paintings and frescos, pestering the mothers and grandmothers of friends—and above all testing and tasting all of these recipes—made me realize that the thread of continuity is even stronger than the differences wrought by time and distance.

The "red revolution"—the invasion of the subtle palette of the Italian larder by the strident colors of tomato and chili in the mid-eighteenth century—certainly affected the visual aspect of Italian cooking but did not eradicate the old ways. The deep earth colors of slow-cooked meat and game, dried beans, and chestnuts combined with the ancient golden warmth of gourd, pumpkin, and quince, co-exist with recent arrivals from the New World: coffee, vanilla, corn, and potatoes. Many traditional recipes are faithful to this pre-pomodoro past—pumpkin tortelloni, pasta with pesto, salsa verde, walnut and garlic sauces, polpettini with parsley and lemon, crostini and focaccie with olive oil and green herbs.

The kitchen as the center of daily life is well depicted in this nicely informal genre painting, The Kitchen of an Italian Villa, *attributed to Michelangelo Cergnozzi.*

Spices are now used less than in the past. When Pellegrino Artusi published his great cookery book, *La Scienza in Cucina e l'Arte di Mangiar Bene* published in 1891—the work did more to bring about the unification of Italy than *I Promessi Sposi*, Cavour, Mazzini, and Garibaldi rolled into one—he spoke with horror of the pungently-flavored recipes in the cookery manuscripts he was collecting. Literary curiosities rather than gastronomic documents, these "outlandish" spiced and sweetened recipes overshadowed the fresh, simple dishes using pulses and vegetables livened with garlic and herbs and sweet or bitter fruit juices, that are a consistent, refreshing presence in these early manuscripts.

Since Artusi's time, historians in France and Italy have published a wealth of material to extend our knowledge of Italian food traditions. Bruno Laurioux, with an assiduity worthy of Poggio, has single-handedly enhanced our understanding of the relationship between Martino and Platina. Martino of Como, cook to the Archbishop of Aquileia in the middle of the 15th century, allowed his friend, Bartolomeo Sacchi (known as Platina) to base his cookery book, *De Honesta Voluptate et Valitudine*, on his own cookery manuscript. Only two copies of the manuscript were thought to exist, but Laurioux has discovered another and analyzed many more derived from Martino's text, putting Platina's popular book in the context of what can now be seen as a considerable body of manuscript material circulating alongside printed texts.

A detailed analysis of these texts can be done with computers, making it possible, at last, to do away with those meaningless generalizations, endlessly repeated, about the popularity or expense of a particular spice. Pepper, for example, is still alleged to have been so expensive and sought after that it was used instead of money. It now seems that pepper was popular, but by no means unusually costly; its price varied, as did that of most spices, at different periods for different reasons. The dictates of fashion certainly came into it. Thus the new technology—the most liberating tool a food historian could hope for, along with the judicious use of a food processor—makes it possible to bring to our plates a sensitive and accurate attempt to understand the gastronomy of the past.

Cooking methods and utensils were different enough to make it quite hard to reproduce in an ordinary domestic kitchen the searing, dry heat of the spit roast, or the mild, slow warmth of dying embers or a cooling brick oven. But we have the advantage when it comes to pies and tarts, which work well in a domestic oven; and gas or electric grills to brown or finish a dish.

The pounding, grinding, and straining which went on to produce spice powders, chopped nuts, purées and creams were all done by hand. Scappi, with his custom-built, "modern" kitchen, had rooms full of mortars and pestles, sieves, strainers, bolting cloths —and a whole hierarchy of kitchen staff to wield them. There is no denying that food prepared with the loving care involved in all this slow pounding, slicing, shredding, and crushing has qualities of flavor and texture that we cannot reproduce with blenders and food processors. But to the tired-woman-in-a-hurry kind of cook, which is what most of us now are, a few kitchen gadgets are a great help.

The recipes in this book are not exact replicas of quaint dishes from the past. They are unashamedly cheerful versions of just a few of the many delicious things eaten by some of the people who enjoyed the pleasures of the table in the two-and-a-half centuries between Francesco Datini and Martha Washington (whose most treasured heirloom was a battered little handwritten book of recipes in the Renaissance style).

I have translated their recipes and done what was needed to present them in an accessible form for today's enthusiastic cooks to use and enjoy. The original texts of the recipes can be read in the books listed in the Bibliography. Some, like the rational, thoughtful Scappi or the fluent, persuasive Castelvetro, need little interpretation, but others, such as the breathless Maria Vittoria or the stream-of-consciousness style of the earlier, anonymous texts, required something of an imaginative leap to convey what was needed to reproduce their splendid cooking.

Every good cook adapts recipes to the taste of his or her household; a passion for basil, or a loathing of turnips will produce an altered version of a dish. If Pius V had loved garlic as much as I do, Scappi would have specified even more of the stuff. But, as I am cooking for myself, and not some dead pope, I can give my own, living versions of past culinary achievements, aiming first and last to please and hoping that this will inspire other cooks to explore in more detail the treasures it has given me so much pleasure to discover.

GILLIAN RILEY, 1993

*Unripe grapes are pounded in a mortar to make Agresto (verjuice),
a sharp, refreshing sauce—soothing to an upset stomach or troubled
liver. From* Tacuinum Sanitatis in Medicina, *an illuminated
health handbook illustrated with miniatures on vellum for the Cerruti
family in Verona in the sixteenth century; now in the
Osterreichischen Nationalbibliothek, Vienna.*

Francesco Datini's

CONVIVIAL GLASS

Broad Beans & Bacon
Leeks in Almond Sauce

"The only time I've ever seen you cheerful… was when we were tasting that red wine, do you remember? You forgot all about your worries…. We laughed and talked all night…"

Francesco Datini (c.1335-1410) was not a happy man. He was not a Humanist either. But he was part of the bedrock on which the Florentine Renaissance was built. He was a tight-lipped, tight-fisted, mean-spirited, and highly successful businessman. He imported and exported the goods that created the wealth of early Quattrocento Florence.

Ser Lapo Mazzei, his closest friend, was a notary who devoted his professional skills to the administration of a charity funded by the church of Santa Maria Novella. Not as well-off as his friend, and with a querulous wife and a great many children, Lapi nonetheless had a capacity for enjoyment. Escaping when he could to the peace and quiet of his small estate outside Florence, he cultivated his little vineyard and garden. He brought back to Florence flasks of fine vintage wine and baskets of fresh, young broad beans "so tender they melt before you can get them into the pot" as even Datini had to admit. The succulent vegetables and good red wine from Lapi's estate never failed to have a happy effect on his lugubrious friend, Datini.

Broad Beans & Bacon

2 lbs. (1 kg) young broad beans
$\frac{1}{4}$ lb. (120 g) unsmoked *pancetta* (see page 91) or fatty bacon, diced
Butter or olive oil
Garlic to taste
Fresh green herbs, in season
A little water

Shell the beans and cook with the bacon and garlic and a little water until tender. Add the oil or butter and herbs and stir well. Serve warm or tepid.

Omit the bacon and add grated Parmesan for a vegetarian version of this dish.

Datini's fine new house took ten years to build, with much confusion of "masters, workmen, labor, lime, sand, stones, shouts, and despair," according to his friend Ser Lapo Mazzei. The airy loggia looking onto the courtyard had fashionable green walls and was a pleasant place in which to entertain friends to light meals off trestle tables, with woven linen cloths and fine glassware. The scene might be similar to this detail from St. Peter Healing Petronilla, *by Sano di Pietro (1406-1481) in the Pinacoteca Nazionale in Siena.*

Leeks being prepared for market, from the Vienna Tacuinum. *Boiled and seasoned with salt and honey, they made an effective cough cure.*

Leeks in Almond Sauce

4 medium-sized leeks
1 cup ground almonds (see page 90)
1 teaspoon Cinnamon Mixture (see page 91)
Crème fraîche

Trim the tough green outer leaves from the leeks. Slice them vertically and wash under running water. Slice across thinly and put in a heavy pan with no extra water. Cover and heat gently until the juices start to flow. If the mixture seems rather thick, add some crème fraîche. Stir well, and cook for a few minutes more.

Serve hot or warm, sprinkled with the Cinnamon Mixture. You can substitute Parmesan for the spices, to give a rich dish.

Probably nothing like this heavily tattooed Young Daughter of the Picts, *by Le Moyne de Morgues (1533-1588), ever came the way of Poggio Bracciolini during his four-year stay in England but she, too, creates an image of an almost "edible woman."*

Poggio Bracciolini's
EDIBLE WOMAN

Salt Cod in Spicy Sauce
Chicken With Verjuice, "Amorosa"

Poggio Bracciolini (1380-1459), a foremost Latin scholar of the Renaissance, was a convivial character, witty, womanizing, and a great gourmet. When, at the ripe age of fifty, he married Viaggia, a girl thirty-three years younger than himself, eyebrows were raised. Yet, after just six months of marriage, he wrote enthusiastically of the charms of his bride. She was like a delicious meal, he said, in which any change or alteration would affect the exquisite balance of the ingredients. The perfect edible woman! Her views were not recorded.

Sixteen years later, a slightly sardonic letter to Bartolomeo Roverella, Archbishop of Ravenna, thanking him for a gift of four salt fish, conjures up a picture of calm domestic harmony with Poggio and Viaggia and their six children enjoying the gift of figs and fish in their comfortable home in Rome.

The fish, *"quod schenales vocant"*, were dried salt cod or stockfish, "hard as lumps of wood, but free of bad flavor, in fact, without much flavor at all... Though very nice as an appetizer, and after all, anything that performs that function cannot be all that bad...."

Salt Cod in Spicy Sauce

2 lbs. (1 kg) dry salt cod (*baccalà* —see page 90)
½ cup each of water, dry white wine, extra virgin
olive oil, white wine vinegar
and bitter orange juice (see page 91) to taste
½ cup ground almonds (see page 90)
8 prunes and 1 tablespoon of raisins, soaked in bitter orange juice
½ teaspoon cinnamon, cloves, and nutmeg
Freshly ground salt and freshly ground black pepper
1 cup chopped fresh herbs (parsley, marjoram, basil, mint)

Bring the soaked fish gently to the boil in just enough water to cover. Turn off the heat and allow to cool. Trim the fish of skin, bones, and any messy-looking bits.

Simmer the liquids with the ground almonds and spices until the sauce is the thickness you like. Add the drained and stoned prunes and raisins and the prepared fish. Simmer very gently on a low heat, covered, or put in a low oven until the flavors have amalgamated (the sharp freshness of the sauce counterbalancing the earthy pungency of the fish and the mellowness of the dried fruit). Serve sprinkled with the herbs and a dash of cinnamon.

An alternative is to make the sauce much thicker, and bake spoonfuls of the mixture in little pastry casings.

Fish was an important item in the Italian diet, especially on Lean days when meat and dairy products were forbidden. This illustration of fishing in the river is from the Tacuinum Sanitatis *in the Casanatense Library in Rome.*

*A Tuscan farm, from a fresco by Ambrogio Lorenzetti (d.1384) painted
in the early fourteenth century. It is one of a series of frescoes in the
Palazzo Publico in Siena, illustrating the virtues of good husbandry.*

Chicken with Verjuice, "Amorosa"

Platina was in Florence on leave of absence from his job as tutor to the Gonzaga children in Mantua when he enjoyed this dish in the house of Poggio Bracciolini. Poggio was by then very old, harassed by the burdens of his job as Chancellor of the Florentine Republic, and annoyed by his children squabbling over their inheritance. It must have been a relief to chat about common interests—food and classical literature—with this pushy but highly intelligent young man, who was later to become the Vatican Librarian.

1 medium-sized free-range chicken, jointed
4 oz. (120 g) *pancetta* or unsmoked fatty bacon (see page 91)
1 lb. (500 g) sour green grapes, gooseberries or
unripe green plums for the verjuice (see page 92)
Fresh mint and parsley, chopped
Salt, freshly ground black pepper, and saffron to taste

Fry the chicken joints and diced bacon in olive oil until golden and half cooked. Crush the sour grapes and strain the juices through a sieve into casserole. Add the chicken. Stir well to dissolve any brown bits and simmer until the chicken is tender. Season with pepper and powdered saffron and check for salt (the bacon may have provided enough). Serve sprinkled with the chopped herbs.

Platina commissioned this fresco by Melozzo da Forlì in 1477 to celebrate
the inauguration of the new Vatican Library by Pope Sixtus IV. Shown
kneeling, but with no false modesty, Platina points proudly to the
dedicatory inscription.

Bartolomeo Platina's

GREAT WHITE DISH

Biancomangiare
Veal Involtini

"Immortal Gods! Was there ever such a cook?" wrote Platina (1428-81) in an emotional outburst at the end of his recipe for *biancomangiare*. After his account of the tedious, and one has to admit, somewhat unrewarding, process of making *biancomangiare*, Platina bursts into enthusiastic praise of his friend Martino, whose recipes surpass those of Apicius, the author of the only surviving information about cooking in ancient Rome.

Martino of Como was cook to the Archbishop of Aquileia in the 1450s. He must have been a remarkable character. Equally at home in the raunchy taverns of Rome and the palace kitchens of fastidious popes and cardinals, Martino made his presence felt. He could discourse for hours on a given gastronomic theme, and provide vast banquets or delicate little intimate suppers at the drop of a hat. Martino must have had considerable generosity of spirit to allow his pushy young friend Platina to circulate in manuscript, and later in print, a version of his own cookery book.

Platina's *De Honesta Voluptate et Valitudine* became the first best-selling cookery book in history. His claim that his generation were better than the ancient authors they revered in at least one thing—cooking—gives an endearing insight into the cheerful enthusiasms of those early Roman Humanists.

Martino was cooking for a prestigious ecclesiastical establishment. Large numbers of important people who expected, and got, the conventional banqueting fare of the time. On his days off, like many cooks, he ate and drank with his friends. The taverns and *bottiglierie* of Rome were, as always, a hot-bed of boisterous, irreverent, and egalitarian ideas. Indiscreet talk about pagan rituals and papal fallibility, along with gossip concerning new sauces and old-fashioned recipes, was not confined to the taverns. Pomponio Leto's Roman Academy, of which the hot-headed Platina was a member, was a group of serious, gentle intellectuals, with a somewhat unworldly enthusiasm for ancient Roman ways.

When Paul II became pope he cast an intolerant eye on their innocent activities and had them imprisoned and tortured in Castel Sant 'Angelo. Platina was rescued by his old pupil and patron, Francesco Gonzaga, now a cardinal in Rome, and wrote his cookery book while recuperating. To Martino's recipes Platina, writing in his elegant Latin, added information about the medical properties of the ingredients and dishes, references to classical authors, and some fairly assiduous name-dropping. It's interesting to compare Martino's recipes with Platina's later versions – the literate amateur clearly does not have the hands-on touch of the master cook.

With Paul II all set for a long and increasingly intolerant pontificate, Platina's future seemed bleak. An intemperate protest at the pope's sacking of his unruly secretariat brought more persecution and imprisonment. Things looked even worse, but on a hot summer night in July 1471 Paul died of apoplexy after overindulging in iced melons in the Vatican gardens. The new pope, Sixtus IV, was well-disposed towards the humanists. Platina, in favor once again, was appointed to the prestigious position of Vatican Librarian, and embarked on a distinguished literary and administrative career, cut short by his death from the plague in 1481 at the age of sixty.

Anguria Turcica.
Citrullen.

Joachim Camerarius the younger (1534-1598) commissioned this
watercolor in Nuremburg in about 1589. Over a century earlier the
well-known properties of the melon—"cold and humid," and hence likely
to provoke serious gastric troubles—had been the cause of the untimely
death of Pope Paul II.

Biancomangiare

A luxurious party dish as well as an easily digested invalid food, it took a lot of hard work to achieve the unearthly whiteness of *biancomangiare*, the quintessential Renaissance dish, in its original form: washing, cleaning, soaking, and pounding the rice; chicken breasts, from a bird killed the same day, poached in skimmed and clarified stock and carefully shredded until "fine as hairs"; almonds, shelled, soaked, peeled, pounded, simmered in the chicken stock and sieved; everything stirred constantly in a brand new, clean pot over a low heat with sugar and rosewater and served up with a painstaking garnish of glistening red pomegranate seeds and cloves. *Biancomangiare* was the loving combination of luxury ingredients and a very labor-intensive preparation. Fortunately, all this can now be achieved in a few minutes, using supermarket provisions and a little imagination.

A free-range chicken breast
$\frac{1}{2}$ cup glutinous rice flour (from a Chinese supermarket)
1 cup almonds (organic are best—see page 91)
1 tablespoon white sugar
Home-made chicken stock
Rosewater (see page 91)
Cinnamon Mixture (see page 91)
Salt and pepper to taste
Pomegranate seeds and whole cloves, as a garnish

Poach a skinned chicken breast in home-made chicken stock until just tender (fifteen minutes should do it) and take it out of the pan. Grind the almonds. Blend the rice flour to a smooth paste with a little cold stock and mix with the almonds. Simmer, stirring all the time, for about ten minutes until cooked. Put this mixture into a blender or food processor with the shredded chicken breast and mix until really smooth. Put back in the pan to warm and flavor with salt, sugar, and rosewater. Garnish with pomegranate seeds, cloves, and a sprinkling of the Cinnamon Mixture. The result should not be sweet, but rather an intriguing, slightly glutinous, delicate, scented cream. *Biancomangiare* has an aromatic, earthy, but interesting texture and flavor which grow on one.

The poultry yard, from the Vienna Tacuinum. *Many recipes for* biancomangiare *specify a chicken killed the same morning, to achieve the fine, almost silky texture required of the simmered and shredded chicken breasts.*

Veal Involtini

12 slices of leg or rump of veal (cut thinly across the grain)
about 6 by 3 inches (150 × 75mm)
2 oz. (60 g) fatty *pancetta* (see page 91), chopped fine
1 teaspoon fennel seeds and
½ teaspoon coarse sea salt crystals pounded together
1 cup chopped fresh parsley and marjoram
1 teaspoon sweet spices (see page 92)

Flatten the meat and sprinkle with the salt and fennel. If the bacon is very salty cut down on the salt. Chop the bacon, herbs and "sweet spices" together until they make an almost creamy paste. Spread some of this on each slice of veal. Roll them up and tie with fine string or secure with toothpicks. Fry the rolls in olive oil or grill on spits over charcoal. Eat at once with a squeeze of bitter orange juice (see page 90).

This idealized maiden, from a fresco by Domenico Ghirlandaio (1449-94) in Santa Maria Novella in Florence, bears symbolic gifts of fruit and wine to celebrate the birth of St. John the Baptist. The flasks are characteristic of Florentine wine production of the time.

A day on the water with friends portrayed by Vittore Carpaccio (c.1460-c.1525), in the early 1490s in Hunting on the Lagoon, *now in the J. Paul Getty Museum in Malibu, California.*

Andrea Mantegna's
DAY TRIP

Stuffed Trout with Lemon
Pumpkin Tortelloni

The eccentric antiquary Felice Feliciano's account of a somewhat wild outing to Lake Garda in 1464 sheds a new and welcoming mellow light on the character of Andrea Mantegna (c.1431-1506). Harsh and quarrelsome he may have been back home in Mantua, but on a day off with his friends, frolicking in the early October sunshine among the ivy-clad ruins, he seems to have shared in the general euphoria induced by the discovery of twenty-two classical inscriptions and the subsequent celebrations with local wine and refreshments.

At one point the party took to a boat, "properly packed with carpets and all kinds of comforts, which we strewed with laurels and other noble leaves, while our leader Samuel played the lute, and we celebrated all the while...."

Lunch at one of the lakeside inns might well have been freshwater sardines, fried and seasoned whith chopped parsley and bitter orange juice, or trout stuffed with lemons from the famous groves of Benaco on the shores of the lake, and herbs from the nearby meadows. Mantegna's trip bore fruit—his own superbly drawn version of Roman inscriptional lettering graces many of his paintings. His Venetian colleagues, the Bellinis and Carpaccio, signed their works in a similar lettering style, on trompe l'œil paper cartouches.

Stuffed Trout with Lemon

This traditional recipe works wonders with farmed trout and looks beautiful with pink salmon trout.

4 pink trout, gutted and boned
1 fresh juicy lemon
4 cloves garlic, chopped
1 cup chopped fresh parsley
Salt and freshly ground black pepper

Grate the peel from the lemon. Pare away and discard the white pith. Slice the flesh, and cut up into small bits. Mix the lemon and grated peel with the chopped garlic and parsley and plenty of salt and pepper. Stuff each fish with some of the mixture and leave to absorb the flavors for a while. Bake for 10 to 15 minutes in a hot oven and eat hot or cold.

JUBILATIO

When Felice Feliciano wrote an account of his euphoric day out with Mantegna in 1464, he headed it JUBILATIO. It is set here in Matthew Carter's titling, Mantinia, based on Mantegna's version of the classical inscriptions they discovered.

In this self-portrait of 1474, Andrea Mantegna looks down with characteristic severity on the pomp and circumstance of the court of the Gonzagas from an architectural detail in one of his frescoes in the Camera Picta of the Ducal Palace in Mantua.

Cabbages and pumpkins (the basis for so many delicious dishes) are piled up in this early seventeenth-century kitchen scene by Astolfo Petrazzi (1579-1665). The cook carries a chicken studded with cloves and the salami glows appetizingly in the foreground.

Pumpkin Tortelloni

This is a speciality of Mantua which Mantegna and his friends may often have enjoyed.

3 free-range eggs
Sufficient flour to make a stiff paste, about $1\frac{1}{2}$ lbs. (750 g)
A well-flavored orange pumpkin, peeled and baked
in the oven in foil
Salt and freshly ground black pepper
Freshly grated Parmesan
Freshly grated nutmeg
Melted butter

Pile the flour on the working surface and make a well in it. Put in the eggs and mix them into the flour, kneading to make a firm paste. Roll this up into a ball and let it rest. Meanwhile, prepare the baked pumpkin—pound it with freshly grated Parmesan, nutmeg, egg, and pepper.

Roll out the ball of dough until it is thin and almost transparent, like best quality chamois. Cut it with a serrated pastry cutter into $1\frac{1}{2}$-inch (38-mm) squares. Place about a teaspoon of filling on each one and fold over diagonally, sealing the edges with pressure from your finger tips so that the filling is securely contained.

With the thumb and first two fingers of the right hand, wrap the triangle of filled pasta round the index finger of your left hand, pressing the two pointed ends to stick firmly together. The result will be a pretty little bonnet shape. Tranquility rather than speed is the essence of this process, best achieved in the relaxed company of friends—as the most delicious home-made pasta still is in Italy today.

Cook the tortelloni in boiling water for a few minutes—they rise to the surface when done. Serve with melted butter and grated Parmesan.

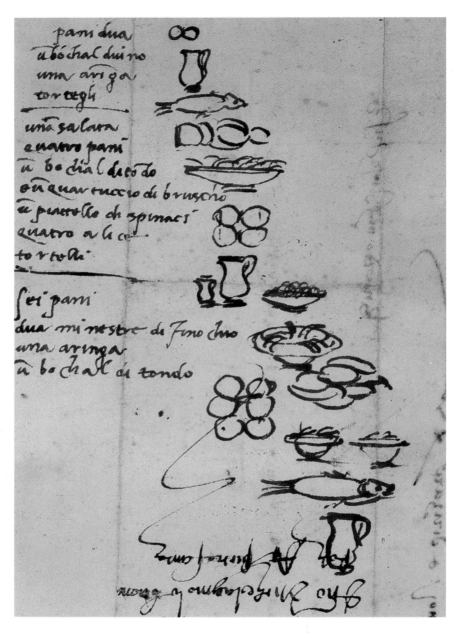

This list of Lenten menus—drawn on the back of a letter sent to Michelangelo in 1517—is amongst the Buonarroti papers now in the Biblioteca Laurenziana in Florence.

Michelangelo Buonarroti's
HOME COMFORTS

Stewed Fennel
Marinated Anchovies
Aromatic Spinach

"...The cats miss you dreadfully and are eating their heads off..." wrote Michelangelo's friend Bartolomeo Angelini from Rome. Detained in Florence on family and professional matters, Michelangelo Buonarroti (1475-1564) missed his comfortable home near the Macel de' Corvi. Florence may have been his native city, but Rome was where his heart lay. He missed his dear friends, Vittoria Colonna and Tommaso de' Cavalieri, his fine house with its terrace overlooking the picturesque ruins of the Forum, the orchard filled with vines and pomegranate trees, and his well-stocked cellar.

What we know about Michelangelo's eating habits is what his biographers Condivi and Vasari told us in his lifetime, with the tacit approval of their subject. Later historians have perpetuated the myth of the rugged genius with his mind on higher things than the gross pleasures of the table or the niceties of clean linen.

But Michelangelo's correspondence shows an interest in the good things of life somehow suppressed by his many biographers. One of his letters has some exquisite little menus drawn on the back, which are often quoted to show how austere and frugal Michelangelo's tastes were. On the contrary, the Lenten fare illustrated here is delicious and well thought out. The spinach and fennel recipes in the monumental cookery book compiled by his contemporary Bartolomeo Scappi, might well have appeared as part of the sumptuous banquets that Michelangelo enjoyed as dining companion to Pope Paul III.

His letters—and Michelangelo never threw *any* of his paperwork away—are full of delightful indications of his appreciation of the little delicacies sent by his nephew Lionardo, and by his many friends: a cartload of Trebbiano wine, a couple of Marzolino cheeses, a nice cured ham, a bag of chickpeas. In return, Michelangelo sent peacock-blue taffeta to a friend's widow, and a diamond and ruby ring for Lionardo's new wife, (along with a most peevish complaint about some shirts, which were not fine enough...).

Throughout the letters kindness and generosity in his response
to little luxuries vie with bouts of titanic exasperation at
stupid blunders—like the flasks of wine that went "off"
during their journey—and rage at the incompetent
business arrangements made
by his feckless
family.

Stewed Fennel

4 medium-sized fennel bulbs
Extra virgin olive oil to taste (see page 91)
Freshly grated Parmesan cheese, about 4 tablespoons
Salt and freshly ground black pepper

Pare away the coarse or discolored parts of the fennel, keeping any fresh green fronds to one side. Wash and chop into chunks the size of your thumb and tip into a heavy-bottomed pan. Sweat the fennel gently in its own juices until soft and tender. (Fashionably underdone vegetables do not, I am happy to say, figure in Renaissance cookbooks.) Add a little water if necessary, to keep it moist; alternatively take off the lid and turn up the heat if it seems too liquid.

When properly cooked, add a seasoning of olive oil, salt, and pepper. Just before serving, stir in the Parmesan and garnish with the chopped green fennel fronds. This tastes best warm.

Fennel, a characteristic flavoring in Florentine cooking, is one of the illustrations in an early sixteenth-century manuscript, Le Livre des Simples Médicines, *in the Bibliothèque Nationale in Paris.*

Even in early old age Michelangelo (1475-1564) had a fine head of dark hair and an austere but kindly expression, as shown in this portrait by Jacopino del Conte, painted in about 1533 and now in the Casa Buonarroti in Florence.

Marinated Anchovies

Michelangelo's salt herrings would have been soaked and steeped in herbs and aromatics. Here is a version using anchovies.

Take a dozen salted whole anchovies, wipe off any salt crystals, and wash in warm water. Remove bones and guts. Dry and lay in a flat dish. Sprinkle with chopped garlic, chopped parsley, and coarsely ground black pepper. Cover with a good quality olive oil, a little fresh lemon juice, and a few raspings of peel. (Don't use your best extra virgin olive oil for this; it would get over whelmed by the pungency of the anchovies.) Marinate in a cool place for several hours or overnight. Michelangelo would have enjoyed his herrings with the un- or under-salted bread still typical of Florence.

Aromatic Spinach

2 to 3 lbs. (1 to 1.5 kg) fresh leaf spinach
$\frac{1}{2}$ cup dried fruit
4 salted whole anchovies
$\frac{1}{2}$ cup pine kernels
Extra virgin olive oil (see page 91)
Salt, pepper, white sugar, and cinnamon to taste
Balsamic vinegar (see page 90)

Wash the spinach leaf by leaf under cold running water (the ultimate test of true affection—a dish to make only for the best of friends). Shake it dry in a lettuce tosser and put it into a large pan. Cover the pan and cook slowly over a low heat, turning gently from time to time, until the leaves wilt.

Meanwhile, rinse any surplus salt from the anchovies and chop them into quarter-inch (6-mm) lengths. Warm them through in a little olive oil. Fry the pine kernels until golden. Soak the dried fruit in a little Balsamic vinegar.

When the spinach is tender but not soggy, pour off any juices (keep them for soup) and stir in the anchovies and their oil, the pine kernels, and the drained fruit. Season with freshly ground black pepper and a sprinkling of Cinnamon Mixture (see page 91).

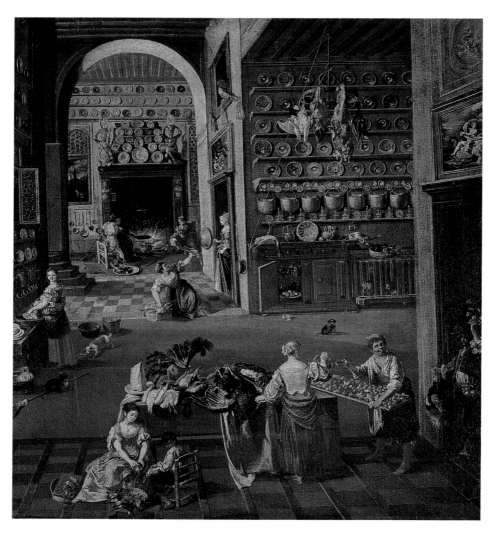

The multifarious activities of a noble kitchen are seen in this seventeenth-century painting by Joseph Heinz the younger in the Museo Davia Bargellini in Bologna. The plucking of fowl and the preparation of vegetables, the cooking of various dishes simultaneously over an open fire, the meat and poultry hanging to the required state of maturity, the normally locked cupboard for spices, wine, and condiments, and the bustle of servants and overseers all add up to a somewhat idealized version of the inferno of a late Renaissance kitchen.

Bartolomeo Scappi's
CORRIDORS OF POWER

Zabaglione

Like Platina's mentor, Martino, Bartolomeo Scappi (c.1500-c.1580) was a professional cook. As chef to the nobility and papacy, he understood just how to cater for intimate little gatherings as well as for the vast state banquets he describes in his monumental *Opera* of 1570.

The pope's banquet, held after Vespers on Friday the 31st of May (the day of Venus) in a garden in Trastevere was a modest little supper for a few friends—about forty of them—with only three courses. The first course offered twenty-six items, from dressed anchovies to fresh strawberries and clotted cream with sugar. The second course was of twenty-four dishes including tender young broad beans in their pods (probably eaten raw with salt), baby artichokes cooked in butter with bitter orange juice and pepper, bite-sized chunks of Parmesan cheese, and fresh green almonds, split and served on vine leaves. The third and final course had eighty-eight bowls and one hundred and twenty-eight dishes filled with candied fruits, preserves, sugared almonds and pine kernels, and boxes of quince paste. The meal was completed with perfumed toothpicks and, for each guest, a posy of silk flowers with golden stems.

In comparison there was a more serious meal, again in Trastevere, offered by Cardinal Lorenzo Campeggio to the Emperor Charles V on the occasion of his entry into Rome in April, 1536. With musical accompaniment, two hundred different dishes were ceremoniously presented to the guests. There were five courses from the sideboard (pre-prepared dishes) and seven from the kitchen. The first service was of thirty-six dishes of biscuits, marzipan, and little tarts of puréed chickpeas and dried fruit. The first service from the kitchen—this being a Lean day—had just

fourteen dishes, mainly fish (including lampreys baked in a pie and cold roast carp dressed with sugar and rosewater).

The second service brought forth fish soups, stews and pies, baked trout with spices, and candied violets in deep fried pastry cases filled with aromatic rice. The third service included sturgeon in white sauce with parsley. Next, from the sideboard, came forty-five different dishes of fruit, nuts, preserves, pastries—and some raw fennel to clear the palate. The table was cleared, bowls of scented water brought to wash the hands, fresh white napkins unfurled, and a new array of dishes brought. Then more from the kitchen: serious grills of tunny, mullet, sole, and a few pies and tarts. Another kitchen service included stewed carp with raisins and fresh herbs, calamari stuffed in the Venetian manner, and a resplendent multicolored jelly. Again from the kitchen a course of baked and roasted fish, hake in a mustard sauce, sea bass in a white sauce decorated with pomegranate seeds, and a cunning counterfeit ham made of salmon in gelatine. The last service from the kitchen consisted of various fried fish, some little plum tarts, and twelve dishes of broccoli served hot with olive oil, bitter orange juice and pepper.

And so the feast progressed. The final course began with a surprise. The new lot of napkins, when unfolded, released flocks flocks of little song birds among the guests, who then tucked into fifty-four bowls of sugared spices and nuts, boxes of fruit jellies, and a golden dish piled high with glistening sugared pomegranate seeds.

The Renaissance Banquet (overleaf) was a political statement, a massive display of conspicuous consumption, a gastronomic assault course, and a challenge to the organizing abilities of the cook. Fortunately the guests were allowed intervals for energetic dancing, theatrical entertainments, music and allegorical pageants—as well as rest periods in private rooms. This extravaganza, from the circle of Pietro Francesco Garoli (1638-1716), is a Baroque version of the traditional Renaissance banquet held in the courtyard of a grandiose palace—where the architectural setting matches the scale of the feast.

Zabaglione

4 fresh egg yolks
4 oz. (120 g) caster sugar
1 cup Marsala, or any sweet aromatic wine
$\frac{1}{2}$ teaspoon cinnamon

Beat the egg yolks and sugar to a foam with the wine and cinnamon. Cook the mixture in a basin over a pan of simmering water until it thickens. Scappi also gives a savory version, using chicken stock and less sugar.

Representations of banquets were originally disguised as religious subjects. It is difficult, in this sixteenth-century painting, Belshazzar's Feast, *from the circle of Andrea Michieli (c.1542-c.1617), to disentangle the religious theme from the trappings of a modern banquet.*

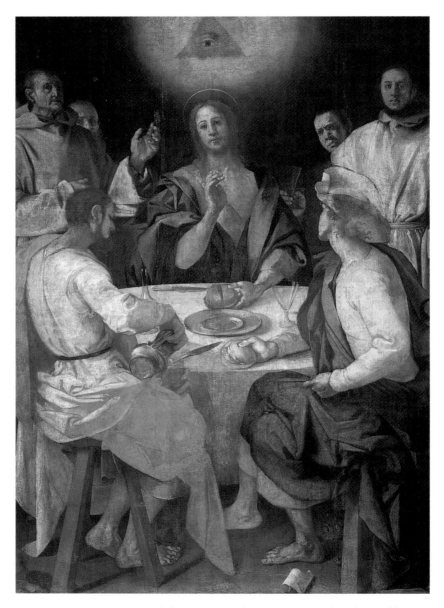

*Pontormo (1494-1556) did not paint food for fun. In fact, the only meal he
described in paint was the ethereal* Supper at Emmaus *in the Uffizi
Gallery in Florence, where the delicacy of his handling of the table linen,
glass, and bread seems to echo his own ascetic tastes.*

Pontormo's
SUNDAY LUNCH WITH BRONZINO

Zucchini Frittata
Almond Frittata

"On Saturday I dined with Piero, fish from the Arno, ricotta, eggs and artichokes. I ate far too much, especially ricotta. Then next day to lunch with Bronzino but no room for any supper, just my luck to overeat...." That was on March 12, 1555. For over a year the Florentine painter Jacopo Carucci da Pontormo (1494-1556/7) had been keeping a diary, recording the progress on his frescoes in the church of San Lorenzo, and noting what he had to eat each day.

Art historians since Vasari have deduced from this diary that Pontormo was a neurotic, obsessive hypochondriac. To us he seems a thoroughly modern creative person, fully into Seasonally Adjusted Disorders and his own version of that current urban myth, the Mediterranean Diet—with its light, lean meat, fish, salad, omelettes, plenty of bread, fresh vegetables, a little cheese occasionally, nuts, and a glass or two of decent local wine.

Not a nine-to-five man, Pontormo might be up before dawn to labor all day without a break on one of his writhing torsos, then go home to a light meal of fresh young peas, an omelette, and some bread. The next day, a change in the weather would find him moping around the house fretting over the paperwork until rescued by Bronzino and dragged off to a cheerful evening with friends in a tavern up by San Miniato. The next morning saw him back at work, hung over and grumpy. The following day was a public holiday, the feast of Corpus Domini, and the occasion for another of Bronzino's lavish lunches and finally, "for supper just an ounce of tart, hardly any meat, and hardly any appetite...."

Twenty years earlier Pontormo had had a house built for himself in Via della Colonna. His bedroom, where he often worked, was up a flight of wooden stairs which could be hauled up by means of a pulley, so keeping importunate clients and friends at bay.

Often quoted as an example of his misanthropy, this precaution now appears a remarkably sane way of handling the freelance lifestyle! He even cooked little meals for himself up there—omelettes (two beaten eggs cooked in a flat frying pan and rolled up like a fish, or seasoned in one of the ways described below). A closer look at the *frittata* might happily free us from the tyranny of the French omelette— soft, bland, and boring. The Italian way is to use eggs as a vehicle for more interesting things—beaten up with breadcrumbs, Parmesan, and spices; fried gently in butter or oil, and served sprinkled with Cinnamon Mixture.

Zucchini Frittata

4 medium-sized zucchini
4 eggs
4 tablespoons of freshly grated Parmesan
2 tablespoons of ground almonds (see page 90)
Nutmeg, salt, and pepper to taste
2 tablespoons of crème fraîche
Chopped garlic

Grate the zucchini on a cheese grater and mix with the other ingredients. Heat the oil in a non-stick or heavy-bottomed 9-inch (22.5-cm) and pour in the mixture. Cook gently on a low heat, taking care not to let it burn or stick. Finish cooking under the grill. When the *frittata* is golden and slightly risen, it should be done. It will be about 1 inch (25 mm) thick, and it won't be folded. It is best to aim at a nice, moist interior. Delicious eaten tepid or cold.

Almond Frittata

For every two eggs take a heaped tablespoon of ground almonds, a level tablespoon of freshly grated Parmesan, and a pinch of salt. Beat well together with a teaspoon of water. Cook in plenty of butter in a heavy 9-inch (22.5-cm) frying pan, finishing off for a few seconds under a hot grill. Sprinkle with another dessertspoon of Parmesan and a generous sprinkling of aromatic Cinnamon Mixture (see page 91). Fold in half, and in half again, and serve sprinkled with bitter orange juice (see page 91) or rosewater (see page 91).

This enigmatic blend of sweet and savory makes an interesting first course. With a little sugar added to the basic mixture, and a smear of home-made orange marmalade before folding, it becomes a pleasant dessert.

These three apples, a fragment of a frieze painted by Tintoretto (1518-94) some time during his work in the Scuola di San Rocco in Venice (from 1565 to the 1580s) are a homely touch amid the grand sweep of one of his vast history paintings.

This late seventeenth-century market scene by Alessandro Magnasco (1667-1749) in the Castello Sforzesco in Milan, has all the attractions of an Italian market today, from the mounds of vegetables to the festoons of salami and sausages, trays of sweetmeats, and little piles of cheeses.

Galileo Galilei's
ASTRONOMICAL BUTCHER'S BILL

Paduan Boiled Meats
Pot Roasted Stuffed Chicken

Galileo Galilei (1564-1642) was already famous as the Professor of Mathematics, Astronomy, and Mechanics at the University of Padua some time before he began his brilliant work on telescopes. Fellow scholars and admirers from the Venetian and Mantuan nobility made their way to his hospitable home, and if a fragment of his household accounts is anything to go by they must have been well looked after. A bill for the period from December 11, 1604 to January 29, 1605 lists "260 lbs. of beef, 83 lbs. of lamb, and 54 lbs. of veal." Flasks of white wine and barrels of red wine were ordered from the Contarini vineyards. Guests brought gifts of sausages and Marzolino cheese.

The butchers' stalls in the market place (detail from page 52).

Paduan Boiled Meats

A traditional Paduan dish—*bollito*—appropriate for large numbers must have been developed early in the city's history. For then, as now, hordes of pilgrims to the cathedral of Saint Anthony, tourists, and students at the University needed to be fed. This version of the rich *bollito* contains beef and chicken.

3 lbs. (1.5 kg) top rump of beef
1 large capon
1 salt beef tongue, previously soaked in water
1 calf's head or cheek
1 large onion
3 stalks celery
2 carrots
2 parsnips
Bay leaves, parsley, garlic, 8 whole cloves, cinnamon, to taste
Serves 8-12

Put the piece of beef in a pot large enough to hold it and the capon comfortably. Cover with cold water and bring gently to the boil. Simmer slowly for two hours. Add the chicken, vegetables, and aromatics and top up with water if necessary. Cook for another two hours, or until the chicken is tender. Meanwhile simmer the tongue for two hours in a separate pot of water. Take it out and cook in a fresh lot of water for another two hours. Cook the split calf's head in the tongue's *first* cooking water until tender.

Carve the beef and the peeled tongue into slices, the chicken into joints, and the calf's cheek into chunks. Arrange on a large serving platter. Moisten with the beef cooking liquid. Serve hot, with Green and Red Sauces (see page 91) and Agliata (see page 90).

Galileo and his friends were unlikely to have enjoyed this with boiled potatoes—they were still a collector's item, grown in pots by botanists who were as wary of their gastronomic possibilities as they were of those good-looking but strange-tasting pomodori. The best accompaniment to a *bollito* is good, homemade bread and a green salad.

Pot Roasted Stuffed Chicken

This countrywoman (opposite), well-shod to survive the rough and tumble of the farm-yard, was a contemporary of Galileo. She is carrying some of Padua's most famous produce—poultry. Here is a recipe from Scappi for one of these celebrated Paduan chickens.

1 free range chicken or capon
4 oz. (120 g) fatty *pancetta* (see page 91)
4 oz. (120 g) prunes
4 oz. (120 g) dried fruit
Cinnamon, ginger, and nutmeg to taste—grind a 1-inch (25-mm) stick of cinnamon, half a nutmeg and $\frac{1}{2}$-inch (12.5-mm) dried ginger together; fresh ginger is better, chopped fine and added on its own
Garlic if you like
$\frac{1}{4}$ teaspoon saffron soaked in hot water (this can be left out)
2 glasses of good dry white wine
1 glass verjuice (see page 92) or bitter orange juice (see page 91) and some of the orange peel

For the stuffing:
1 cup fresh breadcrumbs
$\frac{1}{2}$ cup chopped walnuts or almonds
$\frac{1}{2}$ cup chopped fresh herbs (parsley, marjoram, rosemary)
$\frac{1}{2}$ teaspoon of the spice mixture (above)
1 egg
Lemon juice to taste, and a little grated lemon peel
$\frac{1}{2}$ cup grated cheese, Parmesan or a mild Cheddar
Salt and pepper, and garlic if you like

A countrywoman going to market with some of the poultry for which Padua was famous in the sixteenth century. From a manuscript now in the Museo Civico in Padua.

Moisten the breadcrumbs in a little chicken stock or water and mix with the stuffing ingredients. Taste for seasoning. Stuff into the cavity of the bird. Put the chicken, breast side down, in a heavy casserole and pack the prunes and dried fruit around it with the *pancetta* and the spices and garlic. Pour the wine and verjuice (or bitter orange juice) into the casserole, and a little water to come half way up the chicken. Add a few scrapings of the orange peel. Cover with a tight-fitting lid; if necessary seal it with a flour and water paste or cover the contents with foil or grease-proof paper. Bring to the boil, then simmer gently for $1\frac{1}{2}$ hours, or until the bird is cooked.

Take the bird out and carve it. Put the pieces in a serving dish with spoonfuls of the stuffing and arrange the prunes and bits of fruit and bacon around it. Pour some of the cooking liquid over the chicken and serve hot.

A fresh, fruity young wine is best with this aromatic dish. The sweet-sour spiciness might be rather antagonistic to a fine old wine.

Paſtinaca ſpecies magna radice
lutea dicitur et siſarum et si...
à Sio
Carotta gialla in Candia dicitu...
nomine sclauo
Pitoma marq id est satiua P...
ca seu Paſtinaca ex Alep

This is one of the hundreds of watercolors of plants commissioned by the
naturalist Ulisse Aldrovandi in the sixteenth century, now preserved in
the University Library, Bologna. These "yellow carrots" were cooked
simply by Maria Vittoria della Verde—chopped and simmered in a little
water and seasoned with salt, pepper, Balsamic vinegar, and olive oil.

Maria Vittoria della Verde

GLUTTONY & GODLINESS
IN A PERUGIAN NUNNERY

Almond Cookies
Drowned Ciambelle (Bagels)
Strozzapreti (Priest-stranglers)
Garlic Sauce
Meatballs for the Convent

Portia, the daughter of Fioravante della Verde, entered the convent of San Tommaso in Perugia in 1574 when she was eighteen years old. She died after forty-eight years as a nun of the Dominican order.

In 1583, Portia, now sister Maria Vittoria della Verde (1555-1622), took up her pen and inscribed in her elegant calligraphy the title pages of two notebooks intended for her private devotions and observations on the spiritual life. In one of these her good intentions evaporated in page after page of practical hints and instructions concerning her more down-to-earth interests—needlework and cookery. Maria Vittoria wrote from the heart, with hands-on enthusiasm and a cheerful disregard for grammar and organization. These were, after all, private jottings and aide-memoires, never intended as formal instructions. Embroidery patterns, notes on the day-by-day matters of convent life, and recipes tumble off the pages. Her accomplished script becomes a hurried scrawl as the ideas flood out, full of good humor and enthusiasm.

The convent's archives do not yield any information about Maria Vittoria's activities in the kitchen, whether she toiled away over a hot stove or had an administrative role, but a close study of the recipes shows that she knew what she was talking about. Maria Vittoria must have been a marvelous cook. Her notes are full of small practical hints: how to hold the knife in place with the fingers of one hand while cutting thin slices of meat for *involtini* with the other; how crushing cooked grapes through a sieve works better with one's hands than with a wooden spoon; and that forcing a stiff cream of sweetened ricotta through the holes in a cheese grater gives a pretty effect on the serving dish.

The recipes themselves are delicious: spinach ravioli, with a filling livened with spices, dried fruit and sugar; prunes, cheese and basil in a stuffing for roast pigeons; delicate little meat balls in a sharp, fruity sauce; a spiced sugary omelette folded neatly into four; a humble stew of chick-peas and chestnuts; substantial, rich dumplings with the happy name of *strozzapreti* (priest-stranglers).

This panoramic view of the Tebaide by Gherardo Starnina (1354-1413) has, in the center, an enclosed monastic garden with two brothers tending the herbs which played an essential part in the gastronomic and medical activities of the religious orders.

Almond Cookies

1 cup ground almonds (see page 90)
1 cup flour or more
$\frac{1}{2}$ cup white sugar
$\frac{1}{2}$ cup rosewater (see page 91)
$\frac{1}{2}$ teaspoon ground anise seeds
$\frac{1}{2}$ teaspoon salt
Almond oil and water

Moisten the ground almonds with rosewater and a little water to make a soft paste. Add sugar, salt, anise, and 1 tablespoon of almond oil and mix well. Stir in enough flour to make a paste which is stiff enough to flatten on a floured surface, but not too dry. Cut into shapes with cookie cutters, prick with a skewer, and bake on an oiled tin in a moderate oven for about twenty minutes, until golden and cooked through.

Drowned Ciambelle (Bagels)

1 lb. (500 g) strong white flour
1 teaspoon dried yeast
1 teaspoon ground anise seeds
1 teaspoon salt
1 tablespoon white sugar
Water as required

Knead the flour and yeast with water, salt, and ground anise to make a soft dough. Leave to rise until it has doubled in size. Knock down, then take egg-sized lumps and roll them into strips. Join the ends to make a circle with a hole in the middle. Cook in batches in a large pan of boiling water. When they come to the top they are done. Take them out and leave them to dry in the open air or in an uncovered baking dish in a cool oven. Then bake them in a hot oven for ten minutes.

Strozzapreti (Priest-stranglers)

2 cups fresh white bread crumbs
1 cup, or less, strong white flour
1 teaspoon salt

Soak the breadcrumbs in boiling water. Make a mound of flour with a hole in the middle (as you would do for yeast). Add the bread and mix with a wooden spoon in a large bowl. Add water to make a soft, stiff dough which you then take out and knead with a little flour. Roll out into a fat snake and cut off finger-length pieces and shape them with two fingers against the back of a curved cheese grater. Flour them well as you make them. Cook in boiling water in a big saucepan, but don't boil too fast, or they will sink to the bottom and disintegrate. Cook them just before you want to eat them, or they will get all leathery. Serve covered with sauce or with melted butter and Parmesan.

Garlic Sauce

3 cloves
6 peppercorns
4 cloves garlic
1 cup shelled and peeled walnuts
$\frac{1}{2}$ cup white breadcrumbs soaked in verjuice (see page 92)
or vinegar
$\frac{1}{2}$ teaspoon salt
1 tablespoon olive oil
$\frac{1}{2}$ cup fresh basil leaves
Cinnamon Mixture (see page 91)

Pound all the ingredients together in a mortar or in a food processor, adding extra liquid or oil if required. Garnish with Cinnamon Mixture.

Honey (from a fifteenth-century miniature in a version of the Tacuinum Sanitatis *in the Biblioteca Casanatense in Rome) was often used as a sweetener for dishes rather than that expensive condiment and medicine, sugar.*

Meatballs for the Convent

1 lb. (500 g) rump steak, chopped or minced
1 egg
½ cup chopped *pancetta* (see page 91)
1 or 2 cloves garlic
Salt, peppercorns, coriander seeds—1 teaspoon of each,
ground (reserve 1 teaspoon)
Sage, basil, rosemary
Oil for frying
1 tablespoon bitter orange juice (see page 91)
½ cup stock

Pound all the ingredients together in a mortar or food processor. Form little balls the size of walnuts and roll in flour and the reserved teaspoon of the spices. Fry in oil with the herbs. When nicely browned, add stock and bitter orange juice. Simmer until all the liquid is absorbed. Serve hot.

Nasturtium flowers were used as edible decorations in salads as well as ornamental pot plants. Camerarius, who commissioned this watercolor, was a friend and associate of Aldrovandi and Costanzo Felici and shared their enthusiasm for the accurate recording of plants and flowers.

Costanzo Felici

"BETWEEN A ROCK
AND A HARD PLACE…"

Parsnip Salad/Parsnip Fritters
Raw Salad of Young Vegetables
Turnips Armed in Self-defence
Fish in Rosemary & Ginger Sauce

Costanzo Felici (1525-1585) did not much care for his birthplace, Piobbico, a grim little hamlet perched in a declivity between Monte Nerone and Montiego up in the mountainous regions of the Marche. What could have possessed his forebears to leave civilized, urban Lucca for this place? But here he was, a cultivated doctor and naturalist, dividing his time between his frail old parents in Piobbico and his practice in Rimini.

Felici did his best, keeping in touch with his friend Ulisse Aldrovandi, the great botanist in Bologna, with a series of lively letters, often enclosing seeds, roots, and dried specimens of plants, fossils, and even fish.

One of these letters, on salads, developed from an essay into a full-blown treatise on every edible plant available in Italy at that time; full of fascinating information about vegetables and herbs and how to grow and cook them.

The letters sparkle with little domestic details: the rare fish, left so unwisely on the kitchen table, a prey to one of the cats; Felici's cheerfully fecund wife who sends her love, and a nice cheese, and hopes Aldrovandi's wife will bring forth as many children, but with a bit of luck boys (Felici and Virginia had six daughters); the *"furia delle mie vendemie"*—the frenzy of the grape harvest; and the monster parsnips grown from some Egyptian seed. Here are two of Costanzo Felici's parsnip recipes.

Rapum sessile, album et purpureum.

This elegant pink and white turnip, painted for Aldrovandi, as part of
his botanical collection in Bologna, could have been sliced and eaten raw
with oil and lemon, or cooked as Platina describes, with cheese and spices.

Parsnip Salad

Clean or scrape young parsnips and cook them in a very little water until tender. Dress with extra virgin olive oil and bitter orange juice, seasoned with salt and pepper and some of Cinnamon Mixture (see page 91). Eat cold or tepid.

Parsnip Fritters

With larger parsnips, peel and cook them in the minimum of water. Cut into thick slices lengthways, dip in flour or batter and fry in hot oil or butter. Serve really hot, with a sprinkling of Cinnamon Mixture (see page 91).

Turnips Armed in Self-defence

Platina thought this odd name might be a way of warding off attacks by hungry diners in Rome's busy taverns; but it only made the poor turnips more vulnerable!

Cook turnips until done in very little water. Cut in slices and place in layers in a buttered baking dish, covering each layer with thinly sliced soft cheese (a Fontina or Tallegio would do), a sprinkling of spices, and a few dabs of butter. Bake quickly in a hot oven until the cheese melts and eat at once.

Raw Salad of Young Vegetables

A welcome change from crudités—boring raw vegetables drowned in doubtful dressings.

Take the freshest possible, tender baby artichokes, asparagus, and shelled broad beans. Wash and dry them and trim away any coarse or unsightly bits. Arrange decoratively on separate plates. Guests help themselves to salt, pepper, and extra virgin olive oil—and season the vegetables as they wish. Resist the temptation to tart this up with olives and fiddly bits and pieces; simplicity is all.

This detail from a seventeenth-century family portrait by Carlo Cane (1618-1688), known as The Hunt Picnic, *shows some elaborate mixed salads, a fine pie, and cold meats with lemon slices. The meal is presided over by a matriarchal figure who dominates the gathering.*

Fish in Rosemary & Ginger Sauce

3 lbs. (1.5 kg) fillets sea bream, dover sole, or lemon sole
The bones, heads, and trimmings of the fish
1 cup white wine
1 cup water
1 spring fresh rosemary
1 lump fresh ginger (finger-sized) finely chopped or grated
Salt and pepper
Cinnamon Mixture (see page 91)
Bitter orange juice (see page 91)

Simmer the fish bones with the wine, water, bitter orange juice,
ginger, and rosemary for half an hour. Strain. Poach the fish fillets
gently in the liquid in a large, shallow pan. They should cook in
five to ten minutes. Serve in the sauce, garnished with a sprinkling
of Cinnamon Mixture. If you like a more substantial sauce, thicken
it with ground almonds before cooking the fish.

❧◉❧

*This sea turtle is one of the paintings commissioned by Ulisse Aldrovandi
to illustrate his life's work—a complete description of everything in the
natural world. By 1598 he owned over eight thousand illustrations,
many of which are now in the University Library in Bologna. Some of
these were based on specimens sent by his friend Costanzo Felici.*

This painting by Anthonius Claessins (c.1538-1613), A family saying Grace before the Meal, *in Hall's Croft at Stratford-on-Avon, depicts an uncharacteristically austere attempt at portion control—with reinforcements appearing from the right in the form of a roast chicken.*

Giacomo Castelvetro

SCOLDS THE ENGLISH

Two Ways with Asparagus
Beans for the Dead
Cabbage Stew/Cabbage Salad

"Insalata ben salata
poco aceto e ben oliata."

(Salt the salad quite a lot
Then generous oil put in the pot,
And vinegar, but just a jot.)

"And whosoever transgresses this benign commandment is condemned never to enjoy a decent salad in their life, a fate which I fear lies in store for most of the inhabitants of this kingdom."

Giacomo Castelvetro's (1546-1615) innate tact deserted him when his strictures on the unhealthy eating habits of the British rose to a crescendo in his condemnation of their way of preparing salads. In a little treatise, written in 1612 and dedicated to Lucy, Countess of Bedford, Castelvetro suggested instead the perfect Mediterranean *misticanza*—which followed to the letter his Sacred Law of Salads. This was a mixture of fresh young leaves and shoots of rocket, lettuce, sorrel, chicory, dandelion, and cress dressed in the classic Italian style—scrupulously washed, well-dried, sprinkled with a little salt, and a few drops of vinegar, and then generously seasoned with the finest virgin olive oil.

In his attempt to persuade the English to eat less meat and fewer sweet things, Castelvetro offered seductive little dishes of choice vegetables, simply cooked in water or light stock, and seasoned with butter, cheese and fresh herbs, oil and lemon, or bitter orange juice.

Adriaen Coorte, the seventeenth-century Dutch painter, brilliantly
celebrated the simplicities of everyday things. Successful commercial crops
of asparagus were already appreciated in Holland and Italy, but were just
beginning to flourish in England.

Two Ways with Asparagus

Cut away the hard, woody ends of the asparagus and pare off the skin with a vegetable peeler. Cook in salted water in a flat skillet or saucepan until tender. Drain and eat hot with melted butter and Parmesan. (Put the dish in a hot oven for a minute or two to melt the cheese. It is rather tricky to do this under the grill—the acrid flavor of scorched Parmesan would ruin the dish.)

To enjoy asparagus cold, dress with extra virgin olive oil, salt and pepper, and a little bitter orange juice (see page 91) and eat at room temperature.

Beans for the Dead (Fava de Morti)

1 lb. (500 g) dried broad beans
Bay leaves
4 or 5 big cloves of garlic, smashed
Salt and pepper
Extra virgin olive oil

Soak the beans in water overnight. Next morning drain and put in a pot with fresh water, the garlic, and the bay leaves, and simmer until tender. This may take two or three hours depending on the age of the beans. Add water if necessary, but aim for a thick rather than runny sauce at the end. Season with salt, pepper, and plenty of really good olive oil. Serve with lemon and parsley. This dish is good tepid or at room temperature, and is even better next day.

Cabbage Stew

1 medium-sized hearted cabbage, thinly sliced
Good meat or chicken stock
Hard fat green bacon or *pancetta* (see page 91), chopped
until creamed
1 bunch spinach, washed and chopped
Garlic to taste
Fresh herbs: parsley, thyme, borage, chopped
and mixed with the bacon and garlic
Freshly grated Parmesan
Salt and pepper

Cook the cabbage in a little stock until half done. Add the bacon, herbs, garlic, and chopped spinach. Simmer a little longer, until cooked but not soggy and serve with pepper and Parmesan stirred in at the last minute.

※◎※

This painting of bursting ripe melons and some slices of coppa *(lightly salted, dry-cured pork) is from the circle of Carlo Magini. It illustrates the way Italian meals depend on the superb quality of simple ingredients.*

This splendid cabbage, another item from the Aldrovandi archive in Bologna, can be sliced and cooked simply with garlic and olive oil, or treated to long, slow cooking with bacon, spices, herbs, and wine. It can be a light Lenten dish or a sumptuous winter meal.

Cabbage Salad

Shred a firm, white cabbage very thin. Season with bitter orange juice (see page 91), extra virgin olive oil, salt, and pepper. Add some garlic if you like, or a sprinkling of Cinnamon Mixture (see page 91).

Giovanna Garzoni (1600-1670) took conventional still-life painting and made the genre into something special of her own. Her vibrant fruit and vegetables, with their manic perspectives and surreal backgrounds, are rendered in delicate stippled tempera on parchment. This dish of plums was executed in the 1660s for the Medici family and is now in the Galleria Palatina of the Palazzo Pitti in Florence.

Elinor Fettiplace

ANSWERS BACK

Red & White Apple Jelly
A Fool or Trifle
Artichokes in Cream Sauce

"…boile it till it wamble up like sope suds…" explained Lady Elinor Fettiplace (c.1570-c.1647) in this delectable recipe for apple jelly. Perhaps if Castelvetro had been befriended by her, instead of neglected by the Countess of Bedford, he would have had a less gloomy view of English gastronomy. In the pages of her cookery notebook we find a range of light, fresh dishes using fruit and vegetables in a new style which would have delighted him.

Elinor Fettiplace married, with a decent dowry, into the minor Elizabethan nobility. She, like so many of her contemporaries, was not too grand to play an active part in the cooking, preserving, and presentation of food for her household. The gross meats which so depressed Castelvetro would have been replaced in the banquets she organized—in the splendid new mansion built by her husband on their estate at Sapperton in Gloucestershire—with dishes like Artichokes in Cream Sauce and her delicious trifle.

A dish of fruit by Giovanna Garzoni from the collection of her work in the Galleria Palatina in Florence.

Red & White Apple Jelly

2 lb. (1 kg) good-flavored cooking apples
White sugar—$\frac{1}{2}$ lb. (250 g) per pint (600 ml) of juice

Boil 1 lb. (500g) of unpeeled apples, uncovered, until soft. Strain through muslin in a strainer or colander, resisting the temptation to speed things up by squeezing them. This would make the jelly all cloudy. Meanwhile peel the remaining apples and cook them, tightly covered, until they turn red. This could take forever, but persevere. Strain. To each pint of juice add sugar and boil "till it wamble up like soap suds," Elinor Fettiplace's apt description of the process. When it reaches setting point, pour into a prepared mould or jam jars. Do the same with your red juice. These jellies make a pleasant pudding with *fromage frais* or clotted cream and are excellent with roast pork or lamb. This works even better with quinces.

A Fool or Trifle

4 egg yolks
1 pint (600 ml) warm cream
½ cup white sugar
3 teaspoons rosewater (see page 91)
Nutmeg, freshly grated, to taste
Slices of brioche or sponge cake, or good white bread
Medium dry sherry or Madeira

Lay the bread or cake in your serving dish or bowl and soak in good-quality medium dry sherry or Madeira. Cook the egg yolks in a double boiler with the cream and sugar until the custard thickens—but *does not* boil. Season with the rosewater and nutmeg. Keep stirring until it cools, adding more cream to achieve the consistency you want. Pour over the cake and leave to cool— the longer the better so that the flavors can mingle.

This still life by Osias Beert (c. 1580-1624), shows a young artichoke ready to be eaten, al pinzimino, *and some of the cookies and sweetmeats which became universally popular after the introduction of cheaper sugar in the second half of the sixteenth century.*

This study of three different varieties of artichoke and a rose by
Giovanna Garzoni is also in the Galleria Palatina in Florence. The
vegetable markets of Florence today have an abundance of artichokes—
some so small and tender that they can be eaten raw. With their slightly
tart, fresh flavor, they are very different from the overboiled giants
of conventional menus.

Artichokes in Cream Sauce

6 globe artichokes
½ pint (300 ml) heavy cream
½ teaspoon freshly grated nutmeg
1 blade mace
1 level teaspoon sugar
Salt, pepper, lemon juice to taste
Fresh mint and 2 cloves garlic (if you like)
A knob of butter

Discard the coarse outer leaves of the artichokes, peel the stems and cook the whole heads in salted water—with a little mint and garlic—until tender. Drain and cool. Remove the leaves, scraping away the flesh at the base of each one. Cut off the stems and chop. Keep the bits on one side. Remove the hairy chokes and keep the bottoms. Heat the cream with the spices and sugar until almost boiling, then beat in the butter and add a little lemon juice to taste. Warm the artichoke bottoms through in the sauce, taking care not to boil. Season the flesh from the leaves and warm through. Pile this in the middle of your serving dish and pour the bottoms in their sauce around it. Serve garnished with sprigs of mint.

Johann Walther included products of the New World—corn, squash, and beans—in his composition of fruit and vegetables, painted in 1652 and now in the Bibliothèque Nationale in Paris.

Martha Washington's
AMERICAN CONNECTION

White Broth
Raspberry Cream

By the time Martha Dandridge Custis Washington (1731-1802) was making her mark as America's first First Lady, the battered little cookery manuscript she had inherited in 1749 from the her first husband's mother, Frances Parke Custis, would have seemed quaintly old-fashioned.

This treasured heirloom, according to Karen Hess's 1981 edition of the manuscript volume (containing *A Booke of Cookery* and *A Booke of Sweetmeats)* may have belonged to Lady Berkeley, whose family, the Culpepers, had emigrated to Virginia by the second half of the seventeenth century. It appears to be a fair copy of a collection of recipes put together by a group of housewives during the sixteenth and early seventeenth centuries. Many of these recipes are in the tradition—influenced by Italian styles of cooking—which was a direct link with Platina and Poggio Bracciolini.

Perhaps this would have been a matter of surprise, or even indifference, to Martha Washington's contemporaries. The fashionable housewives of Virginia were cooking in the new French style, using the lush profusion of local produce—the squashes, corn, peppers, beans, and tomatoes of the New World and the imported luxuries of tea, coffee, and cocoa.

But here, in our last recipes, we have a clear reference—by way of seventeenth-century England—to the Renaissance *biancomangiare* in the form of a delicate chicken and almond soup. The exquisite fruit desserts of Elinor Fettiplace, a contemporary of the unknown author of Martha's heirloom, are echoed in a simple Raspberry Cream. Medieval traditions transmitted to the New World by its earliest European immigrants speak of a common culture, just as the cookies and bagels of our Perugian nun now seem equally at home in New England and New York.

White Broth

1 free-range capon
2 pints (1.2 L) chicken stock
1 glass dry white wine
1 blade of mace
5 cloves
A 1-inch (25-mm) stick of cinnamon
1 cup dried fruit (currants and raisins)
1 cup ground almonds (see page 90)
$\frac{1}{2}$ pint (300 ml) heavy cream
3 egg yolks
A little good dry *fino* sherry
Salt and pepper to taste

Cook the capon in the stock with the wine and spices tied in a muslin bag. Soak the dried fruit separately in warm water. When the capon is cooked, in about $1\frac{1}{2}$ hours, remove and set aside. Strain the cooking liquid, discarding the bag of spices, and skim off excess fat. Simmer the stock in a clean pan with the ground almonds until slightly thickened. Beat the cream and eggs together and add gradually to the broth, stirring all the time, on a low heat, until it thickens. Flavor with a very dry *fino* sherry and serve with the soaked currants and raisins and some of the chicken meat, finely chopped. This dish can be made as a soup or, with less liquid, as a chicken stew.

Bernardo's Strozzi's (1581-1644) The Cook, *in the Palazzo Rosso in Genoa, includes turkeys waiting to be plucked. They were known in Europe by the end of the sixteenth century.*

Raspberry Cream

1 pint (600 ml) fresh heavy cream
3 whites of egg
2 blades mace
1 teaspoon grated lemon peel (without pith)
2 oz. (60 g) white sugar
1 lb. (500 g) raspberries

Melt the sugar and raspberries together on a very low heat. Strain through a fine sieve into a bowl and let it cool. Meanwhile bring the cream up to the boil, then take it off the heat. Add, very carefully, the egg whites beaten with a little cold cream and stir gently until the custard thickens—putting the pan back on the heat from time to time to avoid cooling too soon. Put on one side and let it cool, then stir in the raspberry juice. Mix together thoroughly to get an even pink color, or swirl the juice in with the minimum of stirring to create a marbled effect.

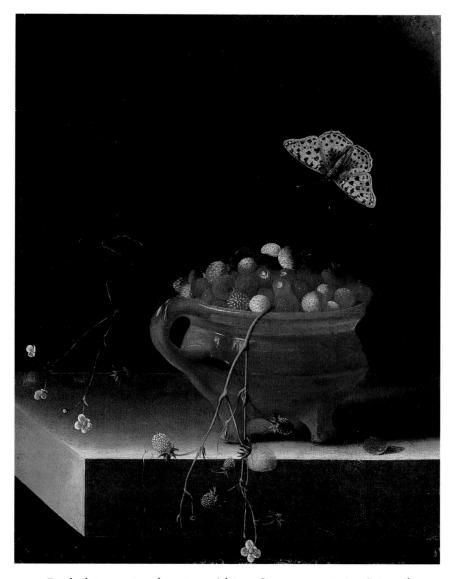

By the late seventeenth century, Adriaen Coorte was painting fruit and
vegetables for clients who wanted his small intimate pictures of familiar
things, without the overload of symbolism found in earlier Dutch still-life
paintings. These strawberries would make a good substitute for
raspberries in Martha Washington's Raspberry Cream.

Glossary & Notes

Old Recipes are like Early Music. We can discover the scores and the recipes, investigate the instruments and the ingredients, but we can never really know what the music sounded like in a certain room, or the taste of the food on a particular plate. When conductors and cooks recreate their versions of past sensations of sound and flavor they add to their scholarship the most potent ingredients of all—imagination and hands-on experience. When using the recipes in this book the reader, will enjoy applying his or her own skills and preferences. Measurements and quantities were not sufficiently standardized in Renaissance cookery for us to lay down precise modern equivalents. Spices and flavorings are especially tricky, and must depend, now as then, on individual tastes. We have scaled our approximate metric renderings down rather than up, giving, for example, 120 g for 4 oz. We have assumed that cups, proportionally used, will give adequate guidance in English or American measures in this context. To simmer a sauce until it thickens is probably safer than guessing at the length of an *Ave*; a knob of butter is going to be the amount you, in prudence or gluttony, wish to add to a dish.

AGLIATA: is a sauce made of garlic, blanched walnuts, breadcrumbs, olive oil, salt, pepper, and a little stock pounded together.

AGRESTO: see VERJUICE.

ALMONDS: figure in many Renaissance recipes, as almond milk (ground almonds soaked in milk or water and cooked until thick, sometimes strained); peeled, skinned, and chopped or ground; roasted dark brown and used to make dark gravies and sauces; or lightly fried and used as a garnish. The business of peeling, chopping and pounding with pestle and mortar is time-consuming but produces an interesting texture. However, where a recipe seems to need a smooth, creamy effect it is sensible to cheat and use a food processor.

BACCALA: Dried salt cod. Not the same as stockfish, which is wind-dried. But both can be used in *baccalà* recipes.

BALSAMIC VINEGAR: is made from the reduced must of grapes and a vinegar starter and matured slowly—sometimes for twenty to thirty years—in barrels of different woods which impart their flavors to the liquid, which becomes ever more concentrated and aromatic.

BITTER ORANGE JUICE: Oranges were mainly the bitter variety—now known as Seville oranges, and sold in Britain in January and February for making marmalade. They can also be bought in Latin American stores in North America. The juice makes a delicious substitute for vinegar in salads, an aromatic marinade, and a refreshing addition to stews and sauces when added just before serving.

CINNAMON MIXTURE: is my version of a spice powder which gives an "Instant Renaissance" flavor to sweet and savory dishes. Pulverize in the coffee grinder 2 inches (50 mm) of cinnamon stick, 1 teaspoon salt crystals, 1 tablespoon caster sugar. Store in a jar in the fridge. A squeeze of bitter orange juice, a sprinkling of rosewater, and a dash of this powder transform a roast chicken, soup, or cooked vegetable salad.

LARD: is not the equivalent of *lardo.* which means bacon, or bacon fat. Commercial lard is bland and tasteless and will not do for frying. Use fat from an aromatic pork roast instead. Good olive oil is a healthy substitute, although giving a different flavor.

OLIVE OIL: when used as a garnish or in dressing should be an extra virgin oil with a flavor appropriate to the dish. Kept in a cool dark place, a selection of these expensive oils can enhance many simple vegetable recipes. For frying or everyday use choose a good blended commercial olive oil, which will be much cheaper.

PANCETTA: Bacon is specified in many recipes, but in most of them the water-logged commercial bacon available today would be a poor substitute for the hard, salted, and cured fatty *pancetta* which can be bought in Italian delicatessens.

PARSNIPS: appeared in many imaginative recipes in the past, but are virtually extinct in Italy today. Having sent them some seeds from England, the Lancellotti family now grow several varieties, and Italian gastronomes beat a path to the door of their restaurant at Soliera, near Modena, to sample traditional dishes made with this exotic root.

ROSEWATER: triple strength, sprinkled on as a seasoning just before serving adds an exotic aroma and enhances the other flavors in a dish. It is important to buy the culinary, not the cosmetic, version.

SAUCES: *Red*—before tomatoes were in common use, a red color was obtained from sandalwood. Scappi made red-currant jelly to use as a garnish, and made a sauce from the remaining pulp, boiled up with wine and a little water, spices, salt, and breadcrumbs or crumbled fig biscuits. *Green*—pound in a mortar, parsley, young spinach leaves, sorrel, rocket, and a little mint; add almonds, walnuts, or breadcrumbs to thicken; season with salt, sugar, and vinegar. I also add olive oil. *White*—see AGLIATA.

SPICES: were used by cooks for pleasure, not to disguise the flavor of tainted meat. Many medieval recipes were pungent and strongly spiced; the lighter cooking of the Renaissance used subtle combinations of spices and herbs, very like styles of "new cuisine" today. The most common spices in Renaissance recipes were cinnamon, nutmeg, cloves, and pepper. Cardamom, cummin, cubebs, long pepper, and grains of paradise were available, but used far less than in the Middle Ages.

Two popular spice mixtures were used in stews and stuffing or added as a garnish: *Strong Spices*—grind together 1 tablespoon black peppercorns, 1 teaspoon cloves, 2 teaspoons cinnamon pieces, $\frac{1}{4}$ teaspoon saffron, and $\frac{1}{2}$ teaspoon dried ginger. *Sweet Spices*—grind together 1 tablespoon cinnamon, 1 teaspoon cloves, $\frac{1}{2}$ of a nutmeg, 1 teaspoon mace, 1 teaspoon dried ginger root, $\frac{1}{2}$ teaspoon saffron, and 1 tablespoon sugar. (See also CINNAMON MIXTURE above.)

SUGAR: White sugar was used more as a flavor enhancer than as a sweetener. Its use comes as something of a shock to us. In the past, however, there was not our rigid distinction between savory and sweet dishes. Banquet menus show meats and sweet things together in the same course. Recipes have sugar and dried fruits in pies and stews, very like some Middle Eastern cuisines today.

TOMATOES: Pomodori were a rare and somewhat suspect import from the New World, grown as decorative pot-plants. "Just a pretty face…" as Costanzo Felici said. Two hundred years later they were to have an indelible impact on Italian cooking.

VERJUICE: in Italian cooking is, in its simplest form, the juice of sour, green grapes, used as a condiment or cooking medium. It can be boiled and fermented, and used throughout the year. The equivalent in English cookery of the past was sour gooseberries, plums, or acidic herbs like sorrel. Turkish cooks still use sour greenish-yellow plums for the same purpose. Now that citrus fruits are cheap and readily available it is simpler to use lemon or bitter orange juice, but it is well worth experimenting with tart fruit, puréed or squeezed onto grills and roasts.

Acknowledgements

The generous support and enthusiasm of three people have made this book possible: Ancilla Antonini of Index; my editor, Treld Pelkey Bicknell; and James Mosley for inscriptions, inspiration, and flowers. If repaid in kind they would be condemned to pass the rest of their lives at a never-ending Renaissance banquet.

Others who helped are: Clive Ackerman, Joanna & Nicolas Barker, Maggie Black, Matthew Carter, Giovanna Casagrande, Andrew Dalby, Alan Davidson, the Gallo Nero delicatessen, the Lancellotti family, Bruno Laurioux, Charles & Veronica Perkins, Hilary Spurling, Maria Raffaella Trabalza, and John Wilkins.

Quotations

I am grateful to Hilary Spurling for permission to quote material from *Elinor Fettiplace's Receipt Book*, Karen Hess for material from *Martha Washington's Booke of Cookery* and Giovanna Casagrande for material from *Gola e Preghiera*.

Illustrations

The author and publishers wish to thank the following for permission to reproduce copyright material: *Biblioteca Universitaria, Bologna* for pp. 58, 68, 71 (Alex Saunderson) and 77; *Christie's Images* for front cover, pp. 9, 25, 44, 45, 47, 66, 74, 76, 81, and 89; *Index* for frontispiece and pp. 12, 15, 27, 70 (© Giancarlo Costa), 19, 64 (Studio Pizzi), 20 (Lensini), 42 (Archivio M.R.), 60, 61 (Galleria Degli Uffizi—P. Tosi) 36, and 57; *Scala* for contents page (detail from *San Giorgio* by Andrea Mantegna, in the Accademia, Venice), back cover, and pp. 14, 22, 29, 33, 34, 40, 48, 52, 54, 82, and 87; *Biblioteca Casanatense, Rome* for page 62 (Alex Saunderson); *FMR* for pp. 78 and 80 (M. Listri); *The J. Paul Getty Museum, Malibu, California*, for page 30; *Yale Center for British Art, Paul Melon Collection* for page 16. Page 51 is courtesy of the *Scuola di San Rocco* (Alex Saunderson); Page 72 is courtesy of the *Shakespeare Birthplace Trust* (Jarrold Publishing); pages 39 and 84 are courtesy of the *Bibliothèque Nationale, Paris*. The Index was prepared by *Atlantic Union*.

❧ *Bibliography* ❧

Anonimo Meridionale, ed. Ingemar Boström. *Due Libri di Cucina*, Stockholm, 1985.

Artusi, Pellegrino, intro. Piero Camporesi. *La Scienza in Cucina e l'Arte di Mangiar Bene*, Torino, 1970.

Barocchi and Ristori. *Il Carteggio di Michelangelo*, Milan, 1965-83.

Black, Maggie. *The Medieval Cookbook*, London, 1992.

Brunetti, Gino. *Cucina Mantovana di Principi e di Popolo*, Mantova, 1963.

Casagrande, Giovanna. *Gola e Preghiera*, Foligno, 1989.

Castelvetro, Giacomo, translated by Gillian Riley. *The Fruit, Herbs & Vegetables of Italy*, London, 1989.

Davidson, Alan. *Mediterranean Seafood*, London, 1972.

Faccioli, Emilio. *L'Arte della Cucina in Italia*, Torino, 1987, 1992.

Felici, Costanzo. *Del'Insalata e Piante che in Qualunque Modo Vengono per Cibo Del'homo*, Urbino, 1986.

Felici, Costanzo, edited by Giorgio Nonni. *Lettere a Ulisse Aldrovandi*, Urbino, 1982.

Firpo, Luigi. *Gastronomia del Rinascimento*, Torino, 1973.

Frati, Ludivico. *Libro di Cucina del Secolo XIV*, Livorno, 1899.

Laurioux, Bruno. *Le Moyen Age à Table*, Paris, 1989.

Hess, Karen, ed. *Martha Washington's Booke of Cookery*, New York, 1981.

Hieatt, Constance B.; Lambert, Carole; Laurioux, Bruno; Pretki, Alix. "Répertoire des Manuscripts Médiévaux Contenant des Recettes Culinaires", in *Du Manuscrit à la Table. Essais sur la Cuisine au Moyen Age*. Montreal—Paris, 1992.

Maffioli, Guiseppe. *La Cucina Padovana*, Padua, 1981.

Messisbugo, Christofaro. *Libro Novo*, Venice, 1557.

Montanari, Massimo. *Convivio Storia e Cultura dei Piaceri della Tavola*, Roma, 1989.

Platina, Bartolomeo, ed. Emilio Faccioli. *Il Piacere Onesto e la Buona Salute*, Torino, 1985.

Origo, Iris. *The Merchant of Prato*, London, 1960.

Pontormo, Jacopo. *Diario*.

Redon, Odile; Sabban, Françoise; Serventi, Silvano. *La Gastronomie au Moyen Age*, Paris, 1991.

Spurling, Hilary. *Elinor Fettiplace's Receipt Book*, London, 1986.

Valerio, Nico. *Mangiare Italiano*, Milan, 1988.

Wardrop, James. *The Script of Humanism*, Oxford, 1963.

The numbers in *italic* refer to illustration captions.

The London Nobody Knows

Written and Illustrated by

Geoffrey S. Fletcher

ARCO PUBLISHING COMPANY, Inc.
New York

Published 1964 in The United States by
ARCO PUBLISHING COMPANY, Inc.
New York N.Y.

Library of Congress Catalog Card Number 64–11058
ARCO Catalog Number 1163

Printed in Great Britain

To my friends

FREDERICK SALFELD
JOHN OLIVER
CHARLES DIMONT
RICHARD BERENS
GERARD FAY

Contents

Introduction

I HAVE no hesitation in admitting that the older I get the more London becomes an obsession with me, so much so that I find myself ill at ease elsewhere, a feeling familiar to Dr. Johnson. It is a good thing, I think, for artists to have an obsession; more than one, indeed, provided that they can all be pursued. The obsession often supplies the driving force for unusual results. Turner, with his preoccupation with light, is a familiar example. Samuel Palmer, in the Shoreham years, was another. The intensity of the Pre-Raphaelites gave a special feverish poetry even to their hangers-on and imitators. Then there was John Martin, a second-rate artist touched for a moment by a weird genius, Fuseli; and Toulouse-Lautrec whose special obsession was the life of Montmartre. Each had his particular *idée fixe*, and declaring mine, I feel myself to be in good company.

When Dr. Johnson remarked that, from the variety of diversions available, a man could avoid an unfortunate marriage more easily in London than anywhere else, he was understating the case. It is my belief that a man can do everything better in London—think better, say his prayers better, eat and cheat better, even enjoy the country better. The country can be graceless and dull and tiresome, as Aubrey Beardsley pointed out, and is, I think, best enjoyed in the imagination or in landscape paintings or on Hampstead Heath. I feel sympathetic to those eighteenth-century poets who dwelt on the delights of a rural retreat, enthused over rustic glades, milkmaids, and swains, without leaving St. James's Street and the Mall. It is possible, anyway, to take long country walks in London, through a chain of parkland and open space, and hardly ever take one's feet off the grass.

You need only visit a secondhand bookshop to be reminded of the innumerable books written about London, and they are still appearing, though how authors continue to find anything new to write about London is a mystery. Many of these books are, however, conventional, even slipshod, affairs, in which the old stuff is brought out time and again for an airing. The old-time Fleet Street journalist I once heard about who made his livelihood solely by retelling old anecdotes and facts about the city culled from Thornbury's *Old and New London* was not exactly unusual. I, for one, am tired of books on London composed of descriptions and illustrations of the Horse Guards, the Abbey, Trafalgar Square, and the Royal Palaces, and although no book can do more than slightly touch on a few aspects of London, I am in this book at least endeavouring to break fresh ground. My theme is off-beat London; the unexplored, unknown-to-the-tourist London. There are whole areas of the capital which are never penetrated except by those who, like myself, are driven on by the mania for exploration: Hoxton, Shoreditch, Stepney, for instance, all of which are full of interest for the perceptive eye, the eye of the connoisseur of well-proportioned though seedy terraces, of enamel advertisements, and cast-iron lavatories.

This does not mean that my concern is entirely with the crummier areas, though these parts of London are given of necessity most attention, since they are precisely the ones lacking appreciation; they are, like the rest of London, changing rapidly, and must therefore be enjoyed while still intact. Neither does the title imply that nothing in my book has ever been mentioned before. My object is to encourage an appreciation of those unlooked-for pleasures of the great city which occur in almost every street and alley, to tempt visitors off the beaten track and to create an enthusiasm for the neglected or undervalued, the freakish, even, if you like. I should be glad to see London explorers boarding buses (and quite positively the best way to see London is from the top of a bus—the pity is that the old open-topped ones were withdrawn) simply because they like the look of the name on the indicator, and to give the well-known sights, which we all know about, a well-earned rest.

This, then, is the obscure, hardly-to-be-thought-of city; the London, very largely, of the hot August pavement and the pleasures of the mean, interminable streets. Gas lamps, a disappearing feature like the horse-drawn van, figure in this saga. Ancient London women with shapeless hats and big feet mournfully appear in this off-beat guide, and totter with heavy bags down area steps. They have the quick dull look of the true Londoner and a wan gaiety which comes from looking at life at uncomfortably close quarters. It is the London of the sleazy snack bar, where the proprietor is not responsible for the loss of any article and where the cups are thick and stamped with the name of a lunatic asylum or perhaps the Bangkok Railway, the patrons being literary gentlemen with a taste for the greyhound section of one of the London evening papers. It is a city that, besides its great Wren churches, has a wonderful collection of cut-price Classical ones; churches in grimy streets possessing perhaps a Burne-Jones window, paper-thin Gothic churches and curious chapels of daft religions without number. I shall ask you to share my fondness for forbidding Victorian flats, for dwelling-houses built for the labouring classes, those to which the unforgettable name of Peabody is firmly attached.

Here and there are dark streets where murders most foul were committed and in which, in spite of the passage of time, one can feel a decided atmosphere—that of Jack the Ripper, the mysterious Peter the Painter, or Dr. Crippen. In this London are cast-iron balconies, exquisitely designed by early nineteenth-century architects, ironwork on which nobody bestows a second glance.

This is the city where one-man barbers' shops are guarded at the door by dreadfully badly drawn figures supposed to resemble men; they are quaint and unnerving like the Jacobean familiars, and bear the legend 'Shave Sir?'. It is the city where the romance of familiar things will be our inexpensive and durable pleasure, the world of the little shop on the corner, the old-fashioned comfortable restaurant and individual fruit pies. It is the place of shabby boarding houses and even shabbier bed-sitters, where the plane tree or lilac surprisingly puts out its leaves in dingy backyards. . . .

There are certain unhappy individuals who take no pleasure in London. Such are frightened by its immensity, a magnitude that emphasizes the emptiness of the heart. The city is too big for them, a mere desert of bricks and mortar. Or else they are dwellers in dormitory areas, dull grey commuters concerned with buying and selling, typing pools and paperwork. London to them is just a place in which to earn a living, and they rarely contribute much of significant value to the capital. People like this, and there are too many of them, desire only to get out of town as soon as possible, and they are destined all their lives to misunderstand the meaning of the city in which they work. They cannot hear the horns of Elfland faintly blowing in Kensington Gardens, haunt of Peter Pan, neither can they see a gaunt figure in an Inverness cape and deerstalker in full cry in Baker Street, nor hear the thrilling command, 'Follow that cab, driver—a life may depend on it!'

In the following pages, we shall embark on unusual wanderings—strange adventures in this reserved, esoteric city, which discloses its secrets only to those worthy of its regard.

Streets Broad and Narrow

ONE OF the many curious things about London is that, whilst it has been well served by poets and artists, it has not been intimately associated with the work of a great artist or poet in the way that Paris of the 1850's is synonymous with Meryon and with Baudelaire. For some reason, no one has dreamed out of London those memorable subjects of architecture, troubled and solemn, fixed unerringly by these artists—Meryon in his etchings, Baudelaire in verse:

'*Souvent, à la clarté rouge d'un réverbère*
Dont le vent bat la flamme et tourmente le verre,
Au cœur d'un vieux faubourg, labyrinthe fangeux
Où l'humanité grouille en ferments orageux,

On voit un chiffonnier qui vient, hochant la tête,
Buttant, et se cognant aux murs comme un poëte,
Et, sans prendre souci des mouchards, ses sujets,
Épanche tout son cœur en glorieux projets.'

London has not as yet inspired such realism, though there is no intrinsic reason why it has not done so. All this is, however (like so much in this book), by the way. The point I am coming to is that Meryon was recording Paris at the right time; whatever may have been the social or political need, the boulevards arbitrarily imposed by Haussmann changed the character of the city. For this reason, London, which owes an immeasurable debt to Wren, was better off without his street plan, drawn up immediately after the Fire; it was logical and arbitrary, like Haussmann's avenues, but out of touch with the genius of the city. Even more out of sympathy are the newer developments in London—the road-widening schemes. Motor traffic is destroying London. Such considerations are not, however, the purpose of this book. I mention them here merely because these roads, lacking the architectural genius of Nash, are eroding the quality of London. Behind these soulless developments looms the city of the machine-made man.

'Let's all go down the Strand' was a popular Victorian ballad. There was some point in doing so then, for it was replete with interest in the form of music halls—the Gaiety and the Tivoli—shops, smoking saloons, the Lowther Arcade and Romano's. Earlier still, in the mid nineteenth century, the Strand still contained much old property, and was considered raffish and rather doubtful. Today it is one of the dullest of the famous streets. Even so there are discoveries to be made. For example, there are a surprising number of ancient houses still left in the Strand. Many of them have been refronted, and it is necessary to see them from the alleyways at the back. Four houses in the Strand retain their ancient fronts and from them it is possible to reconstruct in the imagination a picture of how most of Fleet Street and the Strand looked, as far as domestic houses were concerned, about the time of the Great Fire. Westwards from Temple Bar, there are two forming the Wig and Pen Club, and farther along and opposite Australia House is a pair of charming old houses with overhanging windows surviving from the seventeenth century—Engerts, the photographic dealers, and the premises occupied by the Equity Permanent Building Society. It is not impossible that all these houses date from before the Fire. Near these is the entry that leads to the Roman Bath in Strand Lane, and if you look back in the direction of the Strand, you will see a delightful Regency balcony to a house of the early eighteenth century. This sort of thing goes on all along the Strand. There is the well-proportioned upper part of Thresher and Glenny's, the outfitters, and lower down, on the opposite side above Boots, a bit of 1860-ish Gothic, somewhat in the style of the first Gaiety Theatre which was not far away.

Now I am about to introduce a favourite of mine—though I often tremble for its future—the gas lamp in Carting Lane, by the side of the Savoy. It is almost unique, as only two of these lamps survive in London. This one has been here for about eighty years, and, as can be seen from the illustration, is a superb specimen, richly topped with ornament. It is known as the Patent Sewer Ventilating Lamp; its iron column is hollow to allow, as the name implies, for the passage of sewer vapours. What is more, these gases can be seen in certain lights and smelt too, but not of anything more noxious than cabbage water and the odour of London dinners. It is one of the remaining iron lilies of the Strand. One of the more depressing aspects of old London photographs is to see the abundance of rich gas lamps on the pavements, the crossings and by steps and pubs, for they are now disappearing. On occasions, a rescue operation, as in Trafalgar Square, has been carried out, but then the colour of the gaslight is missing, together with the cosiness of the flame:

'Underneath the gaslight's glitter
Stands a little fragile girl
Heedless of the night winds bitter
As they round about her whirl;

While the hundreds pass unheeding,
In the ev'ning's waning hours,
Still she cries with tearful pleading,
"Won't you buy my pretty flow'rs?"'

Lower down the Strand, and on the other side, is Mooney's Irish House, full of mirrors and gold lettering. A few yards away is a modern building occupied by a shoe firm—Romano House, on the site of the restaurant. I remember Romano's, though not, unfortunately, in its heyday when long ago Romano's shared with the old Café Royal the reputation of being the gayest in town. George Edwardes and his Gaiety girls supped here and poor Bessie Bellwood. Stage-door Johnnies, bookies, and eccentrics were commonplace. Romano's was a sort of clearing house for all the bohemian life of London. There was a tank of goldfish in the window, in which one of the clients relieved himself, no doubt to the despair of the occupants. There was Romano himself, keeping a cagey eye on his more impecunious clients. Phil May was a regular, and often hard up in spite of a prolific output, so the artist often earned his supper by knocking off a drawing on the spot. Gradually the bohemian life of London became watered down, and Romano's entered into a decline. I remember its latter days when only the American Bar remained open. When the end came and the cellar was sold, I went over the building while the breaker's men were in. I stumbled up the stairs to the balcony where King Edward VII, so the foreman told me, liked to have his chair placed in order to watch the dancers on the floor below. The mirrors on the Turkish alcoves were flyblown and cloudy. Striped wallpaper of Edwardian date still covered the walls of the manager's room, and the floor was littered with old dance-cabaret cards and tickets, moved in a melancholy way by a chill wind from the Strand. Downstairs in the kitchens, still with their coke-fired ovens, were two mouldy jars of piccalilli, faithful unto death like the sentinel at Pompeii.

14

*Sewer gas ventilating lamp
in the Savoy*

You will, I hope, begin to appreciate my point about the hidden surfaces of London: turning a stone, one starts a wing. This is by no means all that can be found in the Strand and its tributaries. There is the last fragment of the Adelphi—the fine Regency building that houses the Midland Bank and good enough to be by Decimus Burton—and the group of streets named after the Duke of Buckingham, including Of Alley and Villiers Street, the most uninviting of all the streets, I believe, in Central London, a fishy neon-lit street that seems to be open at all times, like Vanity Fair.

London is not all gold: there are those thoroughfares that are stale, flat, and unprofitable. Grays Inn Road and the Seven Sisters Road are two examples. Euston Road is grim, certainly, but a lot can be extracted from it. The pavements of King's Cross always seem to be sun-baked and full of football crowds, strolling aimlessly, and day trippers from the provinces—mamas with big bottoms, husbands with open-necked shirts and kids; innocents abroad, ready to be fleeced. One of my favourite bits of Edwardiana—Reggiori's Restaurant—has been converted into a snack bar. It used to be a complete period piece with tiled and mirrored walls and those hat stands shaped like a honeysuckle flower. I like the souvenir shops of King's Cross and Euston. Their contents fascinate me—plastic snowstorms of the Abbey, ball-point pens with St. Paul's; I know one shop which displays wonderfully ghastly ties, patterned with striptease girls, and sells itching powder, and plastic cigarette boxes, shaped like altars, which play the 'Ave Maria'. Here be dragons in the shape of London landladies, owners of small hotels ('B. & B.') in the streets off the lower end of Euston Road; we are on the fringe of Bloomsbury, the land of boarding houses.

King's Cross and St. Pancras Stations present in easily appreciated form the cleavage in Victorian architectural thought. Both are, of course, superb. Those great arches spanning the arrival and departure platforms of the old Great Northern Railway are as dramatic as an etching by Piranesi. The clock tower in between is less satisfactory; it is an Italianate motif appearing at this time (about 1851) in market halls; the façade of King's Cross would have been more impressive without it.

St. Pancras gives me endless free entertainment and real pleasure each time I see it. The old story that Sir G. Gilbert Scott, the architect, utilized his rejected design for the Foreign Offices is simply not true. He had long before acquired a knowledge of Continental Gothic, and used it at Exeter College, Oxford in 1858. Still, it is very fortunate for Whitehall that no similar building appeared there, tame as Scott's Government offices eventually became. St. Pancras is a vast wedding-cake assembly of ornament, scenic and cheerful—Euston Road would be very dreary without it. French and Venetian Gothic intermingle to provide a style that is pure Scott. One might truthfully call it Academic Gothic Revival—in other words, eminently able but somehow lacking in enthusiasm. It is worth examining in detail at leisure, admiring the varied skyline, the dormered roof and massive projecting porch, fretful with carved stone and ironwork. It is intensely evocative of the late 1860's, and must have been charming when shining in its new Nottingham brick and Ancaster stone, with crinolined and top-hatted figures emerging from horse-drawn cabs below.

There is not much else to detain the explorer in this part of Euston Road, except (on the side opposite St. Pancras Station) a corner block of the late Regency; it is one of the last relics of the simple Georgian houses built after the street had been laid out as the New Road in the eighteenth century. And there is an early cinema, not quite a collector's piece, but with its old electric lamp brackets remaining.

Euston is too well known to be mentioned at length. Its original simplicity has been overlaid by later additions. The demolition of the great arch and the Great Hall, whether they are preserved elsewhere or not, will be a national loss. Above the Great Hall are rooms of splendid quality, unknown to most travellers, the Shareholders Room and the Board Room of the L.N.W. Railway. The architecture is late Classical Revival, a style favoured by mid-Victorian Bankers. It possesses a massive dignity and inspires confidence. Both these rooms are to disappear; I shall regret the Board Room especially, having a liking for the fireplace of white marble, topped with three busts of the railway giants, Locke and the two Stephensons. Things in England change but slowly; the fireplace still has its Victorian fender and coal scuttle, but the clock, wreathed in laurel, is ticking away the minutes to demolition. One of the nicest bits of Euston is the arched end to the corridor outside the Board Room. It has slender columns of cast iron filled in with glass, and as can be seen in my drawing, gives a view over the old platform sheds built by Charles Fox. You feel as if you were up in a balloon, looking over the chimney pots of Euston, floating aloft with the starlings wheeling in the smoky London sunset. There is more than one sunset here; there is also the sunset of the age of steam when England's prosperity was based on coal.

Here I leave railway architecture for the moment, to return to it later at Camden goods yard. Meanwhile, before quitting Euston, London adventurers should sample Eversholt Street which runs alongside the station up to Mornington Crescent and Sickertian London. There are interesting early nineteenth-century terraced houses, grey with railway dirt. On the edge of the Polygon are many barbers (a lathering of barbers,

Kensalgreen
—Tombs with a view

The monuments and gasometers of Kensal Green

to coin a collective noun), small mixed businesses and cafés. One of my favourite Gothic Revival churches is here, half-way down the street where the original Euston platforms curve away behind a wall. St. Mary the Virgin is cut-price work of 1824. It was designed by the Inwoods who built several churches in St. Pancras, notably the Parish Church in the neo-Grecian Style. St. Mary's is worth a visit: it is the kind of tea-garden Gothic that aroused Pugin to a frenzy, and is, I think, the best example of cardboard medievalism in London. I like it in the same way that I like bad paintings. After the war, I discovered some 'Gothic' patterned wall-papers in bombed-out houses in this part of London, papers contemporaneous with the church and the product of a similar outlook, absurd but disarming.

If you like London junkshops, there are many in this area 'North o' Euston'. One is near St. Mary's. Junk spills out on to the pavement—feeble watercolours, vases of impossible shapes and sinister hues, fans, gramophones, olive-green aspidistra pots (hallmarks of gentility), and books. Among the locals, a natty character in a bowler hat fingers a tray of medals, and somebody buys *The Romance of Primitive Methodism.* . . .

Now we are heading for Paddington and the reaches of the Blue Lamp area. I claim to write on it with authority, since I tramped nearly every inch of it when I lived in Gloucester Place—and that reminds me of a characteristic London feature, the quick transition from a well-off to a seedy area at the drop of a hat. A single street becomes a sort of Mason-Dixon line of demarcation. You could spend a lifetime nosing round Paddington, and still make discoveries. There are the churches, a synagogue, scores of pubs, terraces peeling like the bark of plane trees, Kensal Green . . . one could go on for ever. Paddington Station can be omitted from this survey, but Praed Street is worth a glance. It is unpleasantly named, I think, and is gradually changing its architecture—or what little it had. Jazzy fronts are replacing the decrepit nineteenth-century façades, but the general character of the street, slightly furtive and flashy, remains. Here are wireless shops, gift shops, shops offering you birth-control requisites, and shops for the sale of novels with lurid covers and titles. One can be antiseptically tattooed or can admire the sign of the false tooth hospital—a curved mouth possessing a personality of its own, twisting into a rubbery smile.

In Edgware Road, the old houses have almost gone, but there is a rich supply of delights, architectural and otherwise, as, for instance, Smiths the Butchers, where they take the meat away after the close of the day's business and sell hot salt beef sandwiches and lemon tea until midnight. The Poppy, a choice pub of brick, stone and marble, is a 'must' for period investigators,

Star Street, Paddington; view down an alley

and opposite, on the corner of Harrow Road, the Red Lion still has its huge lamp brackets.

No visit to the Edgware Road could be complete without an inspection of the market in Church Street. A third of the way down on the right-hand side is the portico of a one-time music-hall—The Royal West London. The name has now gone from the cornice along with the royal arms. People used the royal coat of arms pretty freely in the nineteenth century; stricter regulations now prevail. Luckily for London, the old Metropolitan still survives as a music-hall in the Edgware Road, though it is destined to disappear under one of the fearful road schemes. 'The Met.' is pure late Victorian music-hall architecture, with a light touch of Arabesque and a hint of Edwardian *art nouveau* in the female figures.

Off the road are stucco terraces that lead gradually to the more Italian-ate Bayswater, and there are humble little streets like Star Street. This is a perspective of cheaper terraced houses in brick and stucco. Sharp sudden fights blow up here between urchins and between dogs. Children escape by a hairsbreadth from the wheels of cars, and all along the street on summer evenings, elbows can be seen resting on window-ledges, behind the plant pots. In streets like Star Street, all over London, the householders have an eye for growing things. The areas are highly cultivated with ferns, plants, and Virginia creeper. My illustration was a delight to draw; there was speckled laurel in boxes, geraniums and campanula, and the window-ledge of the parlour was heavy with plants in *art nouveau* pots. In this arbour, budgerigars winked beady eyes at the Paddington sky, with musical accom-paniment by the canaries. Lower down the street, the slender tower of St. Michael's rises above the vista of chimney pots—derelict and dating from 1861. On the walls of the houses opposite are the remains of coronation decorations, from which the reds and blues have fled, leaving the royal portraits in an advanced stage of jaundice.

London window-boxes in the humbler streets often have a feature in the way of decoration which occurs again and again—a little wooden gate tacked on in the middle of the box, a curious relic of country life.

Paddington Green is worth a visit. It retains a little of its eighteenth-century charm in the shape of the parish church, *c.* 1790, by a little-known architect, J. Plaw. It is of London stockbrick, and is shaped like a Greek cross with a white painted cupola. The whole thing looks rather attractive, especially in the spring when the trees are speckled with points of green and the tulips are out. The first London buses started here, a connexion that found expression in the ballad of Pretty Polly Perkins. Today, Mrs. Siddons gazes from her pedestal at the buses through the plane trees. On Paddington Green, at the corner of Harrow Road, is the Siddons

22

Gallery. An art gallery is unusual in this part of London. The owner, who retired at the age of ninety a few years ago, was a gentleman of the old school who knew Phil May. It was a pleasure to purchase drawings from his stock (I bought a fine early Turner drawing for a fiver), and there was this piquant contrast between the Edwardian atmosphere of the gallery and the petrol-perfumed Harrow Road outside, where villainous-looking youths lounged about in those crepe-soled shoes affectionately known as brothel-creepers. I used to get a sort of mental picture of Art (draped in flowing robes and armed with a palette) keeping the Philistines at bay, or else—a subject for a classical cartoon—planting a banner on Harrow Road and entitled, 'With the Flag to Paddington Green'.

Beyond the police station, barrack-like and grim, the Harrow Road is lined with terraced houses, covered with cracks like the skin of a crocodile. These terraces of the middle of the nineteenth century are of fine design, but utterly decayed. Cracks in the stucco reveal the brick construction of the pediments, washing dries on balconies and pigeons fly in at the windows of empty houses.

Of all the London cemeteries, Kensal Green, in Paddington, is, I think, the most melancholy. A visit, therefore, is essential to those in search of the more unusual nuances of London. The cemetery was opened in 1833, a product of the movement in favour of something less grotesque and more hygienic than the old churchyards. These churchyards were fat with over-burying, and were the haunt of resurrection men—hence the building of Watch Houses, as at Rotherhithe. Kensal Green is approached by a kind of triumphal arch, and gains a fantastic, extra-depressing quality by the gasworks in the background. When I went there to make the drawing on pages 18–19, a wrestling poster on a near-by wall announced a certain 'Doctor Death' (a hooded figure like a member of the Ku Klux Klan) 'undefeated in a hundred contests'. From the acres of filled-up ground, it is evident that another and more frightening Doctor Death has been undefeated for a much greater number of contests . . . It is a sort of Père Lachaise, a necropolis where the noise of the railway and the gasworks drowns the song of the birds who hop about the obelisks and mausolea. There are areas of rank grass surrounding graves which remain untended as the families have died out, and old tombs of white stone and pink marble. There is the vast Gothic mausoleum of the Molyneux family, 1866, all marble and carving and most depressing. Here lies Sir William Casement under a canopied tomb, supported by turbaned figures, all in a Greco-Egyptian style; ferns grow out of the cracks, and the chains surrounding the tomb are rusting away. Not far from him is William Mulready, the early Victorian painter, and John Philip, another Royal Academician. Among

Euston Roofs

the tombs of Kensal Green can be traced the decay of Classical art, and the rise of Gothic, and also the decline of fine lettering. Here among the leafy avenues, accompanied by the smell of gas, they are awaiting the general resurrection. I imagine them breaking open the costly marble sarco-phagi, products of heart-breaking labours, and stepping out, as the dead do in the pictures by Stanley Spencer, but in straw boaters, and spats, and elastic sided boots. Meanwhile, however, the railway shrieks and clatters, and a blackbird perches on the decayed top of an urn. Blessed are they that are called unto the marriage supper of the Lamb.

2

Limehouse Views

NOT ENOUGH London visitors go east, though there is much of fascinating interest in the vast areas of Stepney, Rotherhithe, Poplar, and all those great industrial parishes of the late eighteenth and nineteenth centuries on the river. The East End is lived in by the friendliest people in London, who learned their lessons the hard way. It is no good going east with the intention of slumming. Eighty years ago, East-Enders seldom found their way beyond Whitechapel; the rest of London was a closed book to them. Even now they live in their own way, and are not likely to be sympathetic to those merely seeking new sensations. In spite of contemporary housing developments which have affected the close family atmosphere of East-End life, there are rich stores of character and traditions still lingering: people and attitudes that Albert Chevalier and Phil May would instantly recognize as material for their art.

By tradition, Limehouse is a Chinese quarter, but, on my visits at least, Chinamen, sinister or otherwise, have failed to show up. My chief pleasures in Limehouse are confined to a small area, centring around the church of St. Anne. The undertaker's opposite the church is a rare example of popular art. Even today, East-End funerals are often florid affairs—it is only a few years ago since I saw a horse-drawn one—but such undertaker's as this illustrated on p. 27 must be becoming rare, so it is worth study. It is hall-marked Victorian. The shop front is highly ornate and painted black, gold, and purple. Two Classical statues hold torches, and there are achievements of arms in the window and also inside the parlour (in view of 'parlour' being derived from the old French *parleor*—to speak—surely a funeral parlour is rather oddly named?). The door announces, 'Superior Funerals at lowest possible charges'. On one side of the window is a mirror on which is painted the most depressing subject possible—a female figure in white holding on (surely not like grim death?) to a stone cross and below her are the waves of a tempestuous sea. Inside the shop are strip lights—the only

26

Rococo in Limehouse : Victorian funeral parlour

innovation to break up the harmony of this splendid period piece—a selection of coffin handles and other ironmongery and a photograph of Limehouse Church. As I looked, a workman, with a mouthful of nails, was hammering at a coffin. An unpleasant, Teutonic thought occurred to me that, at that very moment, the future occupant of the coffin might well be at home enjoying his jellied eels. . . . Undertakers' parlours of such Victorian quality must be enjoyed before it is too late. This one mentioned is, I believe, the best in London. People stare through the windows of undertakers—at what? Unless they are connoisseurs of Victoriana there seems to me little beyond the elaboration of terror and a frowsy dread that has no name.

One could devote a curious day to a tour of London laundries—not the actual laundries in the sunset lands beyond Euston, but the collecting offices. Chinese laundries are still to be found in the East End, though not many. Laundrettes, a choice study in themselves, have taken their place. Of the collecting offices, the Sunlight Laundries, displaying a rising sun and tiles of an intense ultramarine interest me, and needless to say, those displaying the magic word 'Bagwash'. The word, although in a class by itself, is one of those one would like to use for its own sake, irrespective of meaning, simply because they sound interesting. 'Bagwash' is pure East End, and suggests fat old women pushing prams of underwear. Before crossing the road to Limehouse Church, I recommend a look at the Star of the East, a great Gothic pub, full of mirrors and retaining its lamps outside on the pavement.

St. Anne's, Limehouse, was built by Hawksmoor, 1712–30, one of his three churches in the East End which alone make a worth-while pilgrimage; the other two are St. George in the East and Christ Church, Spitalfields. All were begun within a few years of each other. As early as the 1730's, overcrowding had become a characteristic of the East End, a process accelerated in the early nineteenth century by the cutting of the canal and the building of the docks between 1800 and 1830, the demand for unskilled labour and the arrival of Jews and other refugees from Eastern Europe. These three churches were built as necessities, but there is nothing utilitarian about them. Their originality continues to surprise us. Hawksmoor's architecture, imbued with Baroque rhythms, is yet massive and solid, like Johnson's prose. Characteristic of how little we really value them is the fact that, at the time of writing, Christ Church, Spitalfields, is under threat of demolition, though thousands of pounds are uselessly thrown away in every conceivable direction.

A short walk from Limehouse Church brings us to the river. As the Thames seems to appear in every book on London, my references to it will

Baroque in Limehouse:
St. Anne's Church

be few, except when we go to Rotherhithe on the opposite side. But there is no gainsaying the magic of the river described in prose and in paint by Whistler. The Thames, besides being the chief commercial highway of London and the foundation of its importance, is also the tongue of London, by which the city breathes. Air travels on water, and twice each day the river brings in fresh air from Southend, whence goes back the stale air pulled by the ebb tides. Although the river is still picturesque—beautiful, even, at dusk, when the warehouses become tinged with blue and mysterious industrial exhalations form over the river—the Thames must have been glorious in the mid-Victorian period. In those days, as I have seen in old photographs, the Limehouse shore was a place of curious houses and boat-builders' yards, and sailing ships and masts made a sort of petrified forest. A bit of this old property still remains. There are remnants of good houses off the Commercial Road, a bay-windowed one near Limehouse Church and some few dating from the eighteenth century on the edge of the river, adjoining the Bunch of Grapes. Most of the remaining riverside pubs have been remodelled out of recognition, but the Bunch of Grapes still has its cosy back and a verandah from which customers can watch the ships that pass in the night. Dickens knew the pub. He rechristened it 'The Six Jolly Fellowship Porters' in *Our Mutual Friend*, and something of the old romance remains.

Poplar, easily reached from Limehouse, has lost much of its interest. It was a small village up to the building of the East and West India Docks; the *Great Eastern*, a white elephant among ships, was built here. Architecturally, Poplar has a rather low rating. There are the developments in Cubitt Town by Cubitts' great and still flourishing firm who were so active at the opposite side of London in Belgravia. Cubitts were pioneers in the rationalization of building construction, and in various projects such as the rebuilding of Barings Bank, carried out their contracts with a speed and efficiency that still astonishes.

The Queen's Music Hall has now closed. Here variety 'artistes' could be assured of lively, if critical, patronage. An evening at the Queen's was worth the journey, if only for the audience, which was distinctly Hogarthian. Most of the music halls had an official chucker-out, and if I remember rightly, the Queen's was no exception. I think this official wore a boiler suit and hairy cloth cap, and sold ice-cream as a sideline to cool the heads of the restless gods. This and the Bryant and May Match Tax Testimonial fountain in Bow Road were my chief pleasures in the district. Poplar was chosen as the site of a large rebuilding scheme, Lansbury, which I have visited several times. I cannot think of anything more bureaucratic and dismal. The market square, completed about 1951, has a depressing air

30

about it, quite unlike most London markets. The Trinity Congregational Church is tear-stained with streaky dirt, and the Festival Inn belied its name, on my last visit, with peeling stucco and a decaying sign. Still, life in Poplar has something of its old cockney flavour about it. How little things alter in reality was proved by a boy's sailor suit I saw for sale—a new version of those seen in late Victorian photographs and almost identical. Where else could one buy one but in the Victorian East End?

3

Camden Town

IF YOU carry on from Mornington Crescent, at the top of Eversholt Street, a point left in Chapter One, you find yourself beyond Cobden's statue in Camden High Street, in the centre of a rich and strange civilization. Camden Town was laid out at the end of the eighteenth century, and I can never go there without thinking of that apocalyptic description of the railway constructions in *Dombey and Son*. That Dickens did not exaggerate in the least is proved by the drawings by J. C. Bourne made during the construction of the cuttings and embankments from Euston to Chalk Farm and beyond. Some of the houses, then only recently built, are shown on the edge of the earthworks, and there are hordes of men and horses, masses of wood and metal and confusion everywhere—exactly as described by Dickens.

Camden Town, like Rome, has its catacombs; an extensive area underlying the Camden goods yard is honey-combed with them. The goods yard lies west of Camden Town in Chalk Farm Road, and is of unique interest as, besides the tunnels, there is a remarkable memorial to the early railway age in the shape of the Round House. The tunnels belong to the early railway period. Glistening damps steal down the walls. Going through the passages, as can be imagined from the illustration, is an uncanny experience; it is like walking into a drawing by Piranesi. Near by are the old stables, used at present by Gilbeys; only a few railway horses are left here. The tunnels were used for moving the horses to and from their quarters, and ancient notices remain at the entrance. One reads: 'Horses passing through this tunnel must be led by the person in charge of them. Any person neglecting this rule will be discharged.' Another, more sinister, reads: 'Any person found committing a nuisance near the entrance door of the bonded stores or in any part of this tunnel will be prosecuted. By order.' I like that delightful phrase, 'committing a nuisance', and also the more direct, if ungrammatical, version which simply says, 'Commit no nuisance'.

the Catacombs of
Camden Town

The latter is a threat frequently painted on old walls and alleyways in the dock area. But who, I wonder, would want to commit a nuisance *near the entrance door* of a bonded store, and why qualify it by 'near'?

The Round House is the huge circular building that can be seen from the trains going north. It makes an impressive subject, as can be seen from my illustration, forming the background to a vast paved area and rusty metals overgrown with willow-herb. The Round House dates from 1847, and was designed by Stephenson in association with Dockray and Normanville. Its distinctive feature is the vast conical roof of slate supported on twenty-four cast-iron columns. The building was originally a turntable house for locomotives in the days when the expresses prepared for the journey north above the slope running down to Euston. The turntable has gone, but a short section of line is still to be seen. The interior is galleried and that part of the conical roof between the pillars and the walls is supported on huge wooden uprights with tie-beams above. This turntable house is also tunnelled below. A passage led to an inspection pit in the centre of the turntable. The early, almost lyrical, railway age seems very close here; one can easily people the place with side-whiskered men in corduroy and engine-drivers in stove-pipe hats.

I have already said that the disappearance of Euston is a symbol of the end of the great railway age, but there are one or two places still left in London where the period can be felt, and I digress a moment to mention them here. There is, for instance, Old Broad Street Station. Only the Victorians could have built that exterior staircase with stepped ranges of Lombardic arches. The station has a strong nineteenth-century atmosphere, assisted by a model of an old North London Railway locomotive on a delightfully period stand. From Broad Street ran the Richmond branch of the L.N.W.R., electrified before the Great War—that strange railway journey which finds its way by Camden and Hampstead Heath stations to Surrey, the L.N.W.R. (as it was) running on to L.S.W.R. metals at Gunnersbury Junction. Even today (though they will certainly disappear before long), you can occasionally find yourself in an ancient carriage on this line —travelling forward in space, as it were, but backward in time—one of the old carriages equipped with solid woodwork and flyblown photographs that delight the heart of the true collector. Again, there is the curious duality feeling in the atmosphere of Liverpool Street, a grimy Gothic cavern furnished with soup-vending machines and pie-munching travellers, and at Victoria where, having followed the hand pointing out of a cuff into the gentlemen's lavatories, one finds a period door engraved with the words, 'Hats brushed'. St. Marylebone still retains a refined quality about it, despite the ugly modern block clapped on to it at the side. Here there are

The Round House, Chalk Farm

electric lights of the Edwardian period, opaque mirrors, and carafes capped by inverted glasses, but Marylebone Station's most attractive feature is the glass and cast-iron canopy over the entrance. And Finsbury Park on a Saturday afternoon is the last rendezvous of the steam spotters who gather to watch the expresses coming up the hill from King's Cross.

To return to Camden Town. There are attractive terraced streets to be found in the areas off Kentish Town Road, stuccoed houses of the 1830's that have much character about them. Many of these cottages, artisans' houses at the time of erection, are now being restored and sold at fancy prices. London has been gripped by the fever for living in a 'period' house, and some areas, notably Islington, have distinctly gone up in the world. People are prepared to buy houses that, after years of neglect, have to be almost entirely rebuilt, so widespread is the hunger for anything resembling a Regency house, and it is difficult to decide which is going to be the next area for preferment. But if it is sufficiently rotten and decayed, a district is certain to become fashionable.

Another episode in the life of Camden Town is the Greek and Cypriot colony that has built up in recent years. The area around Pratt Street is becoming almost pure Greek; the Greeks were always colonists. Here they have their own church, and run small Greek eating-places and cafés. All this is a reminder that London is a great magnet for provincials and foreigners, people from the ends of the earth, all coming as they have done for centuries to try their fortunes, like Dick Whittington, in the great city. Somehow London has managed to absorb them, and they have left their mark on London in its architecture and street names such as Fournier Street and Mandarin Street.

Camden Town is a place of small shops and mixed businesses. There is a nice one in Pratt Street, a little fish shop which displays large oysters on blue-edged dishes, and the feeling of the owners for decoration is shown in the huge shells that decorate the window, shells that are pink inside like the ears of a white cat, and there are roses made of pink paper. It is no wonder that Sickert found so much material in Camden Town—those dolorous bed-sitters, the damp basement flats when life, seen through lace curtains, is a succession of human feet wearing out the pavement tomorrow and tomorrow and tomorrow. Jellied eels were a staple article of diet in Camden Town and still are, though the best of the jellied eel establishments has disappeared, and instead I have drawn (on page 38) one almost identical across the border in Islington. Eel pie saloons appear to date from the turn of the century; at least, the one I have drawn has ornamental glass windows of the period. The Camden one had posters inside, stuck on the walls with the legend, 'Cups of tea, fresh-brewed, 2d.' I liked the fresh-brewed bit and the '2d' had a figure '2' about three feet high, almost filling the poster. The eating-boxes (similar to the boxes in the chop-houses of Dickens's time) are filled with large women accompanied by abnormally vigorous infants drinking Tizer, lorry-drivers and old, shuffling men with cloth caps. The menu includes hot meat pies on thick plates or you can have pies with mash. This is served with a helping of a livid pale green liquid of unearthly appearance, which stains the potato mash like verdigris. The tiled walls are lined with mirrors and reflect the huge bottles of vinegar and outsize salt cellars that repose on marble tables. Devouring eels is a solemn rite in all the working-class districts of London, and assisting in these rites is a sad-faced man who appears from the rear at intervals carrying an enamel bucket of the green liquid.

He picks his way over the sanded floor to deliver his cargo of fluid at the counter where the pies are dispensed. I strongly recommend a visit to an eel pie saloon for they are one of the few places where the Edwardian working-class life of London survives unchanged; the only innovation is the striplighting in the ceiling.

Parkway forms a connecting link between Camden Town and Regents Park. A small art gallery and an artists' colourman give the street a slight Chelsea-like flavour, but otherwise it is mainly pure Camden, with a picturesque addition in the shape of a pet shop. Off Parkway and running down to Mornington Crescent are several streets of terraced houses, of which Albert Road is the best. They are not of outstanding architectural interest, but Albert Road has some rather nice iron balconies at the first-floor windows. Here the process of resuscitation can be studied at first hand, for there is a 'U' and a 'non-U' part to this street; the expensively restored end is at the junction with Parkway, and as you progress down the street, the houses are cheaper, awaiting restoration. These streets were built as family houses for the middle class, but soon declined as the poorer classes moved into the streets made grimy by the railways. The houses were then divided up into those single bed-sitters of dreary aspect so convincingly recorded by Sickert. In Camden High Street is the focal point of Sickert's work in Camden Town—the Old Bedford, now deserted and awaiting demolition. Its loss as a living music-hall can only be described as a tragic loss to London life. The present Bedford stands on the site of the previous music-hall of that name (the later remodelling of the 1890's amounting to rebuilding), and Sickert painted both. Its exterior is not very exciting, being in that curious compound of Renaissance motifs taken from more than one source that can only be described as late Victorian, a style that appeared in office blocks, pubs, music-halls, and banks all over London during the 1890's. The interior was, however, superb. Lightly draped nymphs of a kind that appeared at the Royal Academy in the days of Onslow Ford supported the arch over the boxes. The front of the circle was elaborate with cupids, masks, and electric torches, and the blue velvet drapery of the boxes was echoed in the plush seats. Mirrors reflected striped wall-paper and gas lights, giving unexpected reflections of audience and architecture, the true Baroque of the music hall. My recollections of the Bedford date from its last days when I used to go up there to draw in the mornings during rehearsal (and noted the curious smell of orange peel that Dickens mentions) or during the performance. We often went up from the Slade. I remember being chucked out for protesting about the use of gold-fish in a conjuring act. I saw George Robey there, almost the last of a great tradition that included Marie Lloyd, Dan Leno, George Lashwood, and

Jellied eel establishment

Champagne Charlie, those artists of timeless artistry who set the cockneys singing. Moreover, there was a freakish quality about many of the turns in the touring companies at the Bedford whose corniness appealed to me: chorus girls dressed as nuns singing the 'Ave Maria' in a blaze of purple light; artistic poses ('Les Nudes') in pink tights; opaque slapstick comedy. Besides the Old Bedford, Camden High Street had another music hall, the Royal Camden at Mornington Crescent. This dates from the turn of the century, and is now used by the B.B.C., at least a better fate than that of the Bedford.

Before leaving Camden, there are one or two more buildings worth looking at. One is almost opposite the Camden Theatre; this is the cigarette factory built in 1926, and quite my favourite among London's many freaks, although there is a cinema on a smaller scale but in an identical style in Islington. How on earth anyone could have selected an Egyptian style for a modern factory is a mystery, unless the huge cats at the entrance—emblems alike of the brand manufactured there and of the Egyptian city of Bubastis—formed a link. At all events, the factory with its coloured reeded decoration and 'Egyptian' style lettering is wonderfully bizarre.* However, it is not without ancestors (English ones, I mean) for emporiums influenced by Egyptian architecture and dating from the Regency period can occasionally be found in country towns, and London had a precedent in the Egyptian Hall, Piccadilly, itself a home of singular entertainments.

Another interesting Inwood church is the Greek church with a semi-circular portico of huge Ionic columns in Camden Street. This part of Camden Town has something of the character of the Bloomsbury squares about it, in a humbler way, aided by the disused burial ground of St. Martin's, off Pratt Street. These disused burial grounds are a feature of London, those in the City being much used by office workers and City sparrows. The Camden burial ground has crumbling Gothic Revival tombs that have an attractive melancholy about them when the irises are in bloom.

Back to the upper end of the High Street, at Parkway is one of the Rowton Houses, in Arlington Street. This one, a giant brick and terracotta structure, dates from 1905. There are six of these in London: the original one built under Lord Rowton's scheme in Vauxhall and others in King's Cross Road, in Hammersmith, Whitechapel and Newington Butts. They all date from the period when London was full of shivering men selling penny toys in the gutters of Holborn and Ludgate Hill, human flotsam and

* The Carreras Factory—Arcadia Works—is now undergoing alterations to become "Arcadia House", and the Egyptian character referred to above is being considerably modified, particularly in the polychrome decoration.

jetsam that snuffled its way, eyes turned permanently downwards, along the London pavements, picking up fag-ends or haunting the garbage bins of Covent Garden. The genuine down-and-outers always preferred the streets as a place to spend the night; generally speaking, only the upper grades of deadbeats—hawkers, outcast clergymen, men on the run from their wives —found their way to Salvation Army or Church Army Hostels or the Rowton Houses. Some slept under the Arches and a few on the Embankment, though the latter was too damp and offered little comfort except for the Silver Lady café, round which a weary queue used to form to collect the mugs of tea, bread and butter, and gaspers. Rowton Houses were for the élite. The original price was sixpence a night, and you could have a cubicle to yourself. The price gradually increased up to a shilling and then three shillings and sixpence. The walls were ornamented with prints and flyblown regulations, the smell was that of scrubbed boards and yellow soap and an air of broken-spirited listlessness hung about the inmates. This, of course, applies to all lodging-houses in London, but my favourites are those of the Salvation Army where the beds have (or had) wonderful Victorian counterpanes in red and white, embroidered with the motto, 'Blood and Fire'. The same slouching humanity lives in them all, spectral and bleary-eyed and with a foxy smell, unable or unwilling to communicate with its fellow members. 'In His own likeness created He them'—words to ponder on in a doss-house. However, things have changed in the deadbeat world, and the latest development is that the Rowton Houses are being up-graded. The one I know best, in King's Cross Road, has been entirely reconstructed. The other five are to follow. Hard benches and cell-like cubicles have given way to television sets and bed-sitting rooms with built-in furniture. The doss house is becoming as out of date as the dinosaur.

4

Islington

ISLINGTON is one of the most fascinating parts of London, and an entire book, let alone a chapter, could easily be given to it. The area has a many-sided character: the fine terraces of Canonbury, those of the rest of Islington, some of which are still neglected, and others forming a sort of new Bloomsbury in character as well as architecture; Victorian Islington; and the contrast between the working classes and the newly established ones who paint or write; and so on.

It is today a little hard to realize that Islington in the mid-eighteenth century was little more than a cluster of houses grouped about the green, with smaller, distant hamlets such as Holloway and Canonbury, and that the lower parts of Islington running into Finsbury had tea gardens and spas, Islington Spa being near the Sadlers Wells Theatre, and Bagnigge Wells on a site now occupied by Cubitts near King's Cross. None the less, if you look attentively at the top storeys of Upper Street, where the road widens and the pavement is stepped, you will see the remains of Georgian brickwork and get a passing impression of Islington as a country village. In fact, Islington retained this integrity to a late period; as recently as the 1880's, people who lived in Islington generally confined their lives to the district.

King's Cross and up Pentonville Road is a good way to tour the area, a part of London given to little ironmongers' shops which still retain the sign of the drysalters' jars, little restaurants like Romano's close to Sadlers Wells (illustration on p. 46), dining-rooms and the like. Romano's Fish Dining and Supper Rooms is very characteristic: note the late Victorian woodwork, the hanging lamp with the globe missing and the lace curtains. Of the several streets worth a visit, I single out Wharton Street, up the hill from King's Cross, and Percy Circus. Wharton Street is almost unspoilt and has pretty Classic villas with gardens of minute proportions, full of roses and scooters. The villas are tiny, with triangular pediments, and have

41

a little frilly ornament in the form of Gothic railings. At the top is Percy Circus, bomb-damaged, but its architectural quality can still be admired. My illustration shows the well-proportioned windows of the Circus and the shapely iron railings that enclose the green in the centre. These squares and circuses with their linked terraces are the logical way of living in cities—if cities are to be agreeable to the eye, that is, and not merely soul-destroying glass and concrete beehives; the squares of London are the city's distinctive contribution to architecture. However, the inhabitants of Percy Circus, who at one time included Lenin, are not greatly influenced by these considerations, and continue to proliferate children, to lean from windows, and to clean scooters, to an accompaniment of noises supplied by cats, dogs, and ice-cream chimes.

Up Pentonville Road and in the area behind is Barnsbury, where the White Conduit Tavern marks the site of White Conduit House, so called from a water conduit that once existed there. White Conduit House was a favourite place of amusement in the eighteenth century; Goldsmith visited it and innumerable London apprentices of the sort immortalized in 'Sally in our Alley'. Here they came to enjoy strolls in the garden walks, drink tea in the arbours and watch the fireworks and balloon ascents. On the way up to Islington, St. James's Church in the Pentonville Road is worth noting; it is a pretty affair in the Adam style and was opened in 1788. Grimaldi, the clown, is buried here. Chapel Market can be reached from Penton Street, turning off Pentonville Road at the Belvedere Tavern. Looking back from here in an autumn dusk there is a strange romantic view of St. Pancras, all pinnacles and towers in a smoky haze, a sort of fantastic Mouse Tower, a Gothic Zion.

Penton Street is itself interesting in having an almost unspoilt London dining-room, one of those with a large hanging lamp and lace-curtained windows. There are still a few to be found in London, including one in King's Road, Chelsea, the latter a homely survivor among much that is merely chi-chi and fashionable. The Penton Street one has the typical fly-blown mirrors reflecting each other into infinity, a clock and wooden eating-boxes with acorn finials that remind one of chapel pews. Round the corner is White Lion Street, from which an alley leads to Chapel Market. This area is full of interest for the London connoisseur, for White Lion Street still retains a few early nineteenth-century shops, well used and authentic and in need of preservation. These shops have their original shutters. What they sold originally is impossible to say, but they belong to the time when apprentices slept under the shop counter and had to take down the shutters for their first job of the day. These shops are less obviously

The iron work of Percy Circus

attractive than those by Cubitt in Woburn Walk, but builders (there is seldom an architect involved) had a feeling for proportion in those days, an instinct for form and for doing the thing in a way most satisfactory to the eye. Even the panels of these shutters have the right relation to each other and to the edges of the wood.

Chapel Market extends to Upper Street and is one of the lesser known among the street markets of London. It is also one of the most interesting. The weeks before Christmas are the best time to go there, for it is then that the market is most fully stocked with fruit, vegetables, poultry, and toys. Here a crowd gathers round a man selling boxes of cheap crackers, and a hawker with several days' growth of beard sells magic mice—white mice which run up and down his greasy sleeves. Those who buy them will find that there is nothing but a mouse of white wax inside the bag; the secret is in the manipulation, that is all. Farther along, a smart-Aleck opens a suit-case full of small envelopes. As a crowd gathers, he puts a pound note into two or three envelopes, shuffles them up and calls out for a sportsman who will give him half a dollar on the chance of striking it rich. Eventually, some-one falls and another; it is interesting to see the furtive way in which the envelopes are opened and the feeble grins at finding a mere charm, a lucky charm, of course. The crowd melts away, and so does the smart-Aleck, richer by two or three quid earned in ten minutes, and so on to the next performance. Weird youths, monstrous growths of city pavements, stare listlessly into radio and jazz shops, youths with white-eyeleted shoes accompanied by their fun-molls. Each couple has horribly pointed shoes that make me think of elves; they twitch epileptically to the sound of jazz oozing from the shop. They are collectors' pieces for a book like this.

Chapel Market has rich colour: the blue-pink of plucked chicken, partridges, and pheasants touched with dull reds and prussian blue and occasionally a black and white hare; then the fish stalls, largely of pearly white from the underbellies of plaice and cod, colour accents being supplied by parsley (sometimes of plastic, occasionally real) and the lobsters. The market spreads into several of the adjoining streets, with more toy stalls, more stalls selling toilet rolls and ball-point pens and more colour that Titian might have envied—the bunches of grapes, loads of apples and brussels sprouts, and the awful dark red that comes off the bloody hands of the man cutting up live eels.

Most of the shops in Chapel Market have been modernized, but a few older ones remain; above them can be seen the brickwork of early nine-teenth-century terraced houses, and there is a Baroque note in the archi-tecture of the Chapel House, half-way down the market.

44

London street markets deserve a book to themselves, especially those in the working-class districts. Some, such as Petticoat Lane and Portobello Road, are too well known for this book, and, in any case, have become somewhat self-conscious—like the so-called Caledonian Market now held in Bermondsey. Still, while I like the bilious jars of pickles and the weary teddy boys, I cannot help regretting the fact that London markets are not what they were. I miss the quacks, for example—particularly those who sported a plastercast of a foot crippled with bunions and the medicine men who displayed testimonials from the crowned heads of Europe; it was surprising that so many people of royal blood were so grateful for corn-cures and bottles of diarrhoea mixture. Such a man was Conrad the Corn King, who had cured thousands of innocent sufferers (as proved by innumerable autographed letters). He had stood, so he said, the London markets for fifty years, and had cured the corns of unfortunates in all walks of life, even those declared by Harley Street specialists to be without hope. In case such corroboration were not enough, he offered to give away genuine Swiss watches (jewelled in every hole and guaranteed for seven years) to those who could prove him wrong. Characters like this and the wheezy fellow whose hacking cough ceased the moment he swallowed a spoonful of his 'Original Cough Mixture' seem to have gone for good; perhaps they could not compete with the National Health Service, or else they had cured all their customers and so spoiled their own pitch? London quacks have not entirely disappeared, however; they have merely undergone a metamorphosis into more fashionable and expensive forms.

The Angel and The Peacock were the two great coaching inns of Islington. Nothing remains of them now. Here at the Angel is Lyons Corner House, part of which can be seen in the drawing on page 66. I am sorry it is now closed, for it was a wonderful period piece (1899 designed by Eedle and Meyers). It has a bulbous cupola, and belongs to the end-of-the-century Baroque, carried out in terracotta, like those two fantastics, the Hotels Russell and Imperial in Russell Square. Islington High Street is a narrow passage running from the lavatory in the middle of the street and continued into Camden Passage. It is worth a visit. At the lower end of the street are a few eighteenth-century houses remaining, with canopied doors. They are now cheap hotels, and one has a garden of the kind mentioned in Paddington, only better. A little waterfall works in the summer time, and there is a rockery and pots of lilies and various statuettes—a symposium of popular art. The High Street and Camden Passage have become a minor Chelsea in the last few years. Only a few shops have their original character, i.e. newsagents, wireless shops, and the like; the antique dealers have moved in on a large scale and the last of the real junk men has disappeared. Although

Romano's dining-rooms in Finsbury

the antique shops represent a purely artificial trend, their presence has resulted in the painting-up of the other shops, giving a more cheerful atmosphere. I often wonder what goes on in the minds of the Islington women, themselves antique, who pause for a moment in front of the antique shops, putting down the bags they carry endlessly up and down. I wonder what they make of the marble busts, greengrocers' tea caddies and Regency clocks. There is no evidence: the old girls pick up their burdens and move on.

One of my favourite emporiums here is Lou's, the secondhand clothes shop. As can be seen in the illustration, it is a handsome shop front, with a nice bit of ironwork to ventilate the fanlight. Lou's is popular with the locals, who make a dead set at second-hand clothes. In fact, this interest in second-hand clothes is food for thought, in view of the prosperity people are supposed to be enjoying. Wild orgies of old-clothes buying takes place at all the rummage sales, including those of such demure parishes as St. Martin-in-the-Fields. The women at Lou's have a trained eye for a bargain, and with exemplary skill disinter the garment from a pile of less eligible toggery. There are more antique shops and then comes Mr. Repuke, the undertaker. Over his door (at the back of the shop) is the splendid glass plate reproduced at the end of the book—a survival from the days of horse-drawn funerals. This black charger has a spirited air about him, as if he had a unicorn somewhere in the family tree or had a crusading ancestor or else, remoter still, one who carried a Sir Galahad in quest of the Holy Grail. Camden Passage teems with life, so that even so grand an undertaker as a funeral carriage master seems out of character: the old women totter up and down with laundry bundles, the Islington kids swarm like ants and there are dogs everywhere, cocking their legs up against the lamp-posts. The alley emerges at a Victorian pub which possesses much good sand-blasted and engraved glass, mahogany bar fittings and exterior elevations of Belgian and Dutch influence—that cheerful bastard style so right for pubs, perfected by the Victorians. There is the birth-control shop, Georgian above and with a wonderful enamel advertisement for female pills, and the snack bars to enliven the scenery round here, but I miss the toy shop. This was at the far end of the passage. The building is still there, bay-windowed and with a gas lamp outside, but the toy shop and dolls' hospital has gone. It had seen the generations come and go. Sixty years and more ago, the larger toys were displayed on the pavement, wooden horses and engines, children's chairs and hoops—iron for the boys, wooden for the girls—toy bassinettes and dolls' mail carts. The shop itself was crammed with toys—forts and lead soldiers, games, jacks-in-boxes, tea-sets and monkeys-on-sticks:

47

'Click, click, I'm a monkey-on-a-stick
And anyone with me can play
And my antics he'll enjoy till he finds a newer toy
Then he'll bid me a polite good-day.'

Facing Islington Green is that most famous of London music-halls, Collins's, only recently closed. Collins's today belongs to the late nineties, but the place was started there thirty years before that by an ex-chimney sweep, Sam Collins, real name Vagg. Only the pub which is part of the building is open at the present time; it has a wonderful collection of theatrical photographs and playbills. Collins's bar inside the music-hall had another collection, equally rich and comprehensive. Those playbills are like messages from a lost world—near in time but as defunct as the baked clay tablets from Babylon. It is amusing to see how the florid tradition of the playbills ('entire disregard of expense') survived as lately as the Great War, for a Collins's bill of this period—featuring Gracie Fields in small letters—offers a 'spectacle of Egypt, the Pyramids by Moonlight, the Sphinx, etc., etc.' The Crummles family would have been perfectly at home at Collins's, right up to its last days. They would have approved the faded golden interior, the fish-tailed gas jets and dusty magnificence. Nor would the other acts on the bill have seemed startling to them, for melodrama was always a strong suit at Collins's, and I have seen some few that could never have appeared anywhere else in this century—tear-jerking pieces somehow misplaced in time. If you felt magnificent, a box was obtainable at Collins's for a few shillings. These were furnished with basket chairs that had seen palmier days, and from a box the evening at the music-hall could be enjoyed in full. Part of the feast was, of course, the audience which was curiously restless. Collins's patrons were given to leaving their seats suddenly for no apparent reason, and parking themselves somewhere else. Others would talk across the rows to friends or produce packets of food. This created I know not what sensations in the mind—only Dickens could describe it— and this lassitude was reinforced by the turns which alternated floosies with melodrama. Somebody who had sung something in Italian (terrific applause) earlier in the bill would reappear on a trick cycle balancing plates on her nose, perhaps, or the man who sang 'Mandalay' in evening dress would turn up later as a drunk in an Irish sketch—but nobody seemed to mind. In the end, a disastrous fire made it impossible to carry on, and Collins's rang down the curtain for the last time, positively the last appearance.

Not far from Collins's is an amusement arcade. There are several in London, all variations on a similar theme and all characteristic of a certain kind of London life. In them are large numbers of pin tables, decorated

48

Lou's second-hand clothes shop, Islington

with scantily dressed females, skyscrapers and other choice decorations of transatlantic influence. Some have one-armed bandits or fruit machines, glittering in chromium plate, and in most the pin tables have alluring names such as Ace High, Big Time, Thrillmaster, Atomic Jackpot and so on. It is a curious fact that the male teenage patrons of amusement arcades have dark hair and wear thick-soled shoes. The youths and their girls (flappers they were called in the 1920's when these arcades began) lounge over the machines, shoving coins in, steadily chewing. Some give up and make for the door, staring at the sky and the reflections in the wet road. They are irresolute, afraid of the labour of thinking what to do next, and join in again for another off-hand session, uncertain, restless, wavering. The Islington arcade was once a cinema. The interior (illustration on p. 51) has fat Tuscan columns and the initials E T on a cartouche, standing, one presumes, for Electric Theatre. The exterior as seen from the street is domed and surmounted by a Classical figure, and the place has been a 'sports garden' since the 1920's. They still have an old mirror bearing the legend

Lingards Tripleodeon Amusement Arcade
& Novelty Show

Free   Admission   Free

'Can't think what tripe le odeon means', says a customer, 'must be just a carnival word.' I gather that he has not had a classical education, a guess which seems proved by his attire as, removing his chin from my shoulder, he heads off into the night, displaying a skull and crossbones painted on his leather jacket and the occult words 'Razzle Dazzle'.

Some areas of Islington were still rural up to about a century ago, and apart from its being a favourite resort for holidaying Londoners—an example set by Queen Elizabeth I—Islington was a place of small dairy farms that supplied London with milk and butter. Its rural situation and closeness to town made the development of Islington inevitable through the eighteenth century. With the nineteenth century, the process quickened. It is not easy to fix a date when Islington degenerated (a tendency that has been reversed in recent years), but the dates of the various Victorian blocks of industrial dwellings give a clue. These are from 1865 onwards. Incidentally, I regret that the L.C.C. has decided to drop the names 'Buildings' and 'Dwellings' from its older type blocks of flats. 'Dwelling' is a word which came into our language at a very early period, but I presume it is

Interior of amusement arcade

not considered smart enough for the touchiness of contemporary taste which is ever ready to disguise anything under a pasteurized euphemism.

Many of Islington's squares and terraces are extremely handsome and often very complete. Duncan Terrace, with the New River flowing below the square, has a distinct Bloomsbury appearance, especially those houses with the stuccoed ground floors. Cloudesley Square and many others are all of merit. The end of this graceful period comes in the mid 1840's with Milner Square, grey and forbidding and of harsh proportions. The grimness of Milner Square ought to be experienced by all in search of the more unusual aspects of London, though it is only fair to record the fact that the square had once a pleasant garden and had a pump from which the inhabitants drew their water as late as the 1870's.

It is to Canonbury, however, that we must turn for architectural quality. The manor passed through several hands into the possession of the Compton family, and great care has been taken by the administrators— the Marquis of Northampton's Trust—to preserve the architecture and the amenities of the area. To walk from Upper Street into the nineteenth-century Canonbury Square and so on to Canonbury Tower is to move into an entirely different world, one of those transformations with which London abounds. Canonbury Tower was originally a monastic foundation, and a cloistered seclusion can still be enjoyed in its garden, where fantailed pigeons walk on a terrace, stained in the autumn by the fruit of an old mulberry tree, and the goldfish flash in the pool where the fountain plays. Elegance is the word to describe Canonbury, and the same feeling is carried into the smaller cottage villas and the connecting streets. This quality is only approached, as far as Islington is concerned, by a small area near Richmond Avenue, near that delightful pub, The Albion, and also by Duncan Terrace, and only rivalled by the little squares of Hampstead. Before leaving Canonbury, the Canonbury Tavern, opposite the tower, is worth seeing; it is one of the few remaining London pubs with a tea garden still intact.

5

Iron and Marble

I HAVE always been a keen connoisseur of Victorian lavatories, and consider myself an experienced conveniologist, i.e. one who appreciates their aesthetic qualities. London has a select number of them, though there is an ever-present danger of their modernization and consequent loss of character. Some of the small ones of cast iron are of a high artistic quality and form part of the symposium of London's metallic pleasures, the extent of which will be indicated in this chapter. The men's lavatory in Holborn, which still retains its fine gas lamp in the street above, dates from 1897, and is one of the few with the original fittings. The interior is somewhat cavernous and gloomy, and the roof, cast iron and stained with glistening orange patches, is supported on iron columns sprung from the mosaic floor. Lavatories are solemn places. They are, perhaps, the only true democracy, for in them all men are equal in the sight of the lavatory attendant. Many of these places for standing room only have exceptional collections of graffiti engraved on the walls, particularly those where the stalls are of slate. Such scratchings are worth a book to themselves; no doubt somebody will devote one to the subject sooner or later. Drawings on lavatory walls have an ancient lineage, and were found at Pompeii. In passing, it is worth noting the universality of these drawings; I mean, in style. This applies not only all over London, but also to the rest of the British Isles and all over the Continent; all the drawings might have been done by one man. This, of course, points to something basic in the lower recesses of the human mind—paleolithic, if you like—but why the drawings are so alike in style is to me a mystery. It is not easy to throw light on the problem, in view of the difficulty in obtaining information as to the artists; they have an objection, like the elves in fairy tales, to being seen at work. The urge to express oneself on the walls of a public urinal is worth further study; it differs materially from that which obtains a cheap immortality by carving on the walls of other public build-

53

ings or that of prisoners in the Tower who occupied themselves in this way to pass away time. In this connexion, it is worth adding that, as the months passed towards the outbreak of the last war, the scribblings in London lavatories gradually became more belligerous. This was most notable in the larger conveniences such as those at Hyde Park Corner, and perhaps represent the folk mind letting loose the dogs of war.

To return to Holborn. I made friends with the attendant while I made the drawing illustrated here, and on my pointing out the resemblance of the water tanks to fish tanks, he told me, to my delight, that a previous attendant had actually used them for this purpose. It seemed to me that the fish must have been surprised to find their breathing space restricted and themselves coming down in the world each time the stalls were flushed, and what they made of the copper ball tap in their water I could not imagine. However, keeping fish in a lavatory tank is a delightfully rococo, or rather *fin de siècle*, idea, and might be copied with decorative results. There is also a certain logic about it which appeals to me, and it is wonderfully intriguing to imagine what the men using the place thought of the fish; more important, what the fish thought of the men. My attendant friend told me that there were very few old lavatories left in London (fewer still even today in the West End where the great landowners frowned on them). He called old conveniences 'Queen Victorias', a somewhat startling terminology. I was told that 'the lavatory in Charing Cross Road was the place to go if you want the writing on the wall . . . make your blood run cold, it would.' Charing Cross Road had been cleaned up before my tour of inspection, and so I found no writing on the wall. This lavatory, on an isolated site, is marked by one of the most splendid gas lamps in London, painted in black and gold and equalled only by the lamp at the back of St. Clement Danes in the Strand and the pair in Trafalgar Square; the last, however, are now electrified. Holborn remains one of my favourites, for the gas jets are still intact over the water closets, and there are electric bulbs of Edwardian date which bend over like white tulips. The lavatory at the junction of Kings Cross Road and Pentonville Road was once, I believe, like the one in Rosebery Avenue, a privately owned affair—an odd way to make a living.

Yet another interesting lavatory is the one opposite the Brompton Oratory. From the isolation of the centre of the road, the ironwork makes a foreground to a view of the Italianate Oratory, dating from 1878. (Brompton Oratory is a sort of pastiche of Italian Baroque, built out of hard stone of an unsympathetic quality, but the front is interesting with its narthex and trumpeting angels. Seen in the fading light of a grey autumn evening with the lavatory rails in front, it creates a curious sensation, but under

Sept 1897

S.S. Mutchell
Holborn Feb/64

Interior of Holborn lavatory

these conditions, the church is more attractive, a sort of Canaletto-like view strayed somehow into London.) The lavatory is reached by steep, narrow stairs, and the 'conveniences' inside are of boldly marked marble in brown and white. A tiled frieze of yellow-green acanthus runs above the white tile walls. These classical motifs have been made to suit some unusual purposes since they first saw the light of day, purposes that would have caused some consternation to the designers of the Periclean age. The Victorians were strong minded enough not to bother their heads over incongruous ornament, and made the Victorian lavatory, if not a thing of beauty, certainly a joy for ever. This Brompton one has a mosaic floor with a running leaf pattern in the border that gives one the feeling of behaving rather too freely in some corner of the Alhambra or in some delicately glimmering room in old Bagdad.

Other touches that give the place a comfortable period flavour are the cast iron plates fixed in the walls, with a hand pointing the way out. I like those pointing Victorian hands, often showing a nice bit of linen cuff, which showed (or shewed) so many ways to so many Victorians. They invariably occur in advertisements for patent medicines and cocoa, where the hand points to a warning against fraudulent imitations. The attendant's room has the windows covered with that transparent oiled paper in imitation of stained glass, which was a characteristic invention of the Victorians who were addicted to semblances and simulations. Over the door, is the final touch, a lace curtain—a badge, like the aspidistra, of conformity and utter respectability.

The cast-iron lavatories of London (I mean those entirely of cast iron, of the type illustrated on p. 59, drawn in Star Yard, Holborn) are very decorative. This example has an intricate pattern of ornament to offset the starkness of this strictly utilitarian structure, providing standing room only. The royal coat of arms appears in several of the panels; no doubt, the manu-facturers had a royal warrant for their other productions—greenhouses, perhaps. Birmingham and the surrounding Black Country was the home of these iron conveniences, and they are all of them more solid than their slight French counterparts. One can never hope to see in London the little scene enacted so often in Paris—a man inside the lavatory carrying on a conversation with his girl friend on the outside, a scene at once both logical and stimulating. There are several of these lavatories remaining in London, most frequently down dark alleys, lit by the zinc yellow light of a gas lamp, the whole scene being unchanged from the period of Jack the Ripper and the Houndsditch murders (of which more in a succeeding chapter), a relic of the days when London policemen had walrus moustaches and hearts of gold. Probably the greatest aesthetic pleasure is obtained from the cast-iron urinal at the far end of Cheyne Walk. This also is lit by a ghostly gas lamp, and behind are the curious assemblage of boats, converted wartime craft, ancient Thames barges and the like, that house the floating Bohemian population of Chelsea. This lavatory is also best seen at night and in the autumn, outlined against the plane trees and shining oily river.

In passing, in the drawing of Star Yard, note the bollard making the passage one for pedestrians only. A large number of these bollards remain in London. Traditionally, they are supposed to be made out of old cannon; certainly they resemble the business end of a six-pounder, and no doubt some were just that. There are four in Upper Thames Street by the side of All Hallows the Less that are obviously sawn-off cannon. Most, however, are specially cast and are often of simple dignified design. Designs vary considerably in general. The bollards date from the early nineteenth to the early twentieth century, with some later examples of the 1920's, the latter much less attractive. Many have the initials of the parish cast on them in the bold lettering known as 'Elephant', a favourite type with the printers of playbills in the 1820's and 1830's.

My next illustration—the lamp and clock at the Angel—is what Lewis Carroll might have termed a portmanteau drawing, inasmuch as it comprises several favourite motifs of mine in one subject. These cast-iron public clocks were once a feature of city life, and there are two remaining in inner London—the one at the Angel and the other, more splendid, atop the men's lavatories at Victoria, at the corner of Victoria Street and the Vauxhall Bridge Road. The one at Victoria is a never-failing source of pleasure to me, so debased is my taste; it is a sort of reduced version of Big Ben and, like its prototype, is rich with Perpendicular ornament, thin buttresses, rectangular panels, pinnacles that do no work and an illuminated clock. Such Gothic follies outraged Pugin and the serious-minded Revivalist architects. No doubt, they are also considered beneath contempt by the present-day exponents of faceless office blocks and other modern madnesses, but cast-iron clocks add a lot of fun to the streets. In fact, cast iron always does. In Paris, for instance, the *art nouveau* entrances to the Metro (designed by Hector Guimard at the turn of the century) continually surprise. Lissom and ductile, the metal seems to grow from the pavement like some unhealthy plant in a Beardsley drawing, in the languorous curves of a paragraph by Oscar Wilde. London is short of this scenic metal work and also that of the type represented by the Marché aux Fleurs and the caryatid fountains given to the city by Sir Richard Wallace.

The drawing of the Angel has, besides the clock tower, a very fine Victorian lamp and an architectural curiosity (at least as regards Islington) in the shape of Lyons Angel Corner House previously mentioned. The building is no longer used, but at the time of erection must have brought a touch of Baroque to the lives of the Islington customers, a feeling of having sneaked into a palace in order to consume a cup of char and a penny bun. Lyons no longer concentrate on backgrounds of veined marble, gilt and mirror, but some of their Corner Houses still retain much of it and subdued lighting, too, in the taste of the twenties and the thirties. Certain of the Corner Houses are so eloquent of the nineteen-twenties as to require a label such as 'Late Debroy Somers', just as the exterior of the Dorchester Hotel and the inside and outside of the *Daily Telegraph* building inevitably belong to the period I call 'Early (or Middle) Henry Hall'. This architecture of the twenties and thirties is too interesting a subject to be dismissed in a few lines. Perhaps someone will devote a book to it under some such title as 'The Jazz Age Architecture of London' and elucidate the mysteries of sunray and scalloped decoration and explain why the English steered clear of Cubism when offered in the form of easel paintings but promptly accepted it on cheap suburban wall-papers and watered down on textile motifs and pointless architectural decorations. The Angel Corner House with its cupola and cupids is a cheerful affair.

The pierced pie-crust edge of the lamp is very satisfying. There were a considerable number of lamps like these in the Inner Circle of Regents Park, though of an earlier period; the standards remain, and the new tops, electrified, speak volumes about the poverty of present-day attempts at lamp design; a meanness of execution and material is made more noticeable when the intention is to produce a lamp conforming to a Victorian pattern. The Angel lamp is solid and sturdy, as is the column from which it springs, this being a standard decorated with delicately cast leaves and sunken panels. The chains (reminiscent of a gas bracket in a Victorian parlour) made the work of the lamplighter easier . . . the lamplighter! All the comfort of upper-class childhood in late Victorian London is contained in the word; jellies and mahogany, first party dresses, fog in the Square! Lamplighters are a dying race—not quite gone, like the muffin men, but almost. I hope they survive a little while longer.

58

Star Yard, Holborn

'Now Tom would be a driver and Maria go to sea,
And my papa's a banker and as rich as he can be;
But I, when I am stronger and can choose what I'm to do,
O Leerie, I'll go round at night and light the lamps with you!'

I must not omit to mention the fine pair of lamps in Charlotte Street, near Bertorelli's, and the two in Breams Buildings off Chancery Lane.

At one time, as I have already mentioned, the London streets had a wondrous collection of lamps of all sorts, including those suspended from public houses and shops. These were heavy lamps that required a team of men to install them, with a fixing deep into the brickwork. Pharmacies in particular favoured them; of those still remaining, the one outside Meacher, Higgins and Thomas in Crawford Street, Marylebone, is a fine specimen, with panes of red, yellow and blue glass. The next illustration is of the lamp on Islington Green. In its heyday, this must have been very satisfying to look upon, though it is composed of very simple elements—a deep plinth, a few mouldings, curving leaves of acanthus and a pattern of smaller leaves below the fluted stem. The last-century iron founders could do this sort of thing easily. Compare this with the poverty-stricken ones recently erected in various parts of Westminster, pathetic affairs which, incidentally, displaced in the parish of St. Martin-in-the-Fields those charming lamps, sixty-odd-years-old ones, which had the cartouche of St. Martin dividing his cloak with the beggar—a pleasing touch impossible today. In front of the Islington Green lamp is a horse trough, itself a relic of a vanished age. These troughs, often with a biblical inscription, were installed all over London. One or two are still used—for example, the trough on Euston Road by the side of St. Pancras station and, more particularly, the beautifully kept cattle trough in Wellington Place, St. John's Wood. Beautifully kept because the brass work is always polished and the water clean and, on winter mornings, a man arrives on a bicycle, armed with a long pole which he uses to break up the ice that has formed on the surface of the water. Wellington Place is also fortunate enough to possess one of the elegant Victorian letter boxes of London. These pillar-boxes were not only fine in themselves, they were also admirably adapted to harmonize with Georgian, Regency and neo-Classic terraces and villas. To post a letter bearing one of the 'penny reds' of the sixties in one of these boxes was to correspond in style. The invention of the pillar-box is often popularly, but erroneously, ascribed to Trollope. Actually the novelist did not invent the letter-box, but he is officially regarded as having introduced it into the British Postal Service. Long before then, boxes had been used in Paris for the collection of letters, so there was nothing new in the idea when they appeared here in

1852, the first being put up in Jersey and Guernsey. These were of very simple design. London's first six boxes appeared in 1855; the first one was erected at the corner of Fleet Street and Farringdon Street in the spring of that year. It was reproduced in the *Illustrated London News* on March 24th, 1855, and the caption described it as 'a stove-like design, reminding one of the latest of the London conduits'. These boxes *were* rather stove-like, and had a curving, domed top with a radiating pattern of palm leaves. Such boxes have long since disappeared, but there is a box in similar style resembling an old register stove, only taller, at Waterloo; this, however, is Edwardian.

Before the advent of the boxes, letters were collected by bellmen, who, like the lamplighters, muffin and piemen, were once a familiar sight in the streets of London. The bellmen carried portable letter-boxes, and people posted a letter and at the same time pressed a coin into the bellman's hand. An ingenious scheme, I fancy, this giving to a letter-box the means of locomotion. In 1856 came the fantastic boxes designed by the Science and Art Department; these were heavily encrusted with ribands, classical leaves and national emblems. They were overdone exactly as, in inverse ratio, modern boxes are underdone. Here and there in London are the survivors of the nineteenth-century round-headed boxes with a rosette top and bottom—there is one in St. George's Square, Pimlico—and one or two freak designs appeared in London in the earlier years, but failed to win acceptance. With the sixties, however, the finest box of all emerged, and most of the Victorian letter-boxes of London are of this kind—the Penfold type of 1865, designed by J. H. Penfold. The Wellington Place box is of this sort, and there are others in the East End, in York Gate, Regent's Park, in Camden Town and Kensington High Street and elsewhere in London. Unfortunately, the Post Office, which preserves as many as possible in use, has no complete list, but others remain in various parts of the country as this design was adopted as a general standard. Penfold's design is preserved in the Post Office archives, the box being topped by a crown, a device which was finally modified by the acorn-like finial. The Penfold boxes are hexagonal on plan, and have a refinement and distinction which makes them a joy to see. It is hard to understand why the Post Office ever replaced them by the types in use today, of which the later nineteenth-century box in South Lambeth Road is an early example. Or why, for that matter, the Penfold boxes cannot be reintroduced, to add pleasure to our rapidly deteriorating townscapes. The 1865 boxes were cast by Cochrane, Grove & Company of Dudley. In going through the voluminous files of correspondence in the Post Office archives, I was interested to find an invoice sent by the foundry to 'Mr. Trollope, surveyor for Northern

District, Ireland', written in a flowery hand and pricing their boxes at £7 18s. 3d. It is not generally the policy of the Post Office to interfere with them, and, in fact, in a few places, when the question of a replacement has arisen, the public has shown itself strongly in favour of preservation, so there are grounds for hoping these boxes will continue to decorate the London pavements.

I have said that London is not well supplied with decorative ironwork, but there is, of course, the delightful Albert Suspension Bridge, a choice example of Victoriana, and in the City, the Leadenhall Market. Part of the market can be seen in the illustration of its public house, in Chapter 8, and it is worth visiting as a complete period piece. In fact, all the London markets ought to be included in the itinerary of those seeking the unusual qualities of London: Billingsgate where the fishy smell has sunk into the very pavements, Covent Garden in the early morning, a scene of apparently inextricable confusion, or the fruit and vegetable market in the grimy Georgian streets near the Southwark Cathedral, or Smithfield in late December. Leadenhall Market is built on land purchased from Sir Richard Whittington, and the market has been held since the early fifteenth century. The present market dates from 1881 and is perhaps best approached from its main entrance in Gracechurch Street. Poultry and dairy products are its main business. Leadenhall Market is solid and reassuring, and it asserts the Victorians' belief in the virtues of cast iron. The entire market with its adjoining alleys is of the greatest interest to the London virtuoso. The ironwork is highly elaborated with ornament and the griffins which support the City's coat of arms, the colour scheme being yellow, dull red and gold —discreetly sober. One of the most attractive buildings is the Lamb Tavern, on page 113, with its large hanging lamps and engraved glass. All is Victorian here, apart from the human element and the delivery vans. Large policemen are a feature of Leadenhall Market, and cockney women, authentic Gerts and Daisies, are to be found rubbing shoulders with city gents taking the air at lunch-time. There are modern versions of Young Smallweed, old, old men with years of smoking behind them and the butchers whose bald heads shine under the electric lights. If the butchers' and poulterers' shops are like a Dutch still-life, the gardening and seed shops (especially in the spring) are reminiscent of the brilliant intricacy of colour found in an early Millais. People slowly circle round the flowering standard cherries and rose bushes, meditating over boxes of herbaceous perennials. It is always good to see these green border plants in the dusty heart of the City in spring. (You can smell as well as see and feel the coming of the spring to London.)

Snack bars are an essential item in and around Leadenhall Market,

Lamp standard and horse trough, Islington

and the market men and van drivers are on easy terms with the waitresses and proprietors who supply inexhaustible quantities of tea. Other shops include small newsagents, Dowlings Restaurant, drawing attention to itself by a hand pointing to the interior where marble-topped tables are still in use, and a pet stores. Here are the various plastic toys which the English believe to be a source of amusement to budgerigars: there is something touching in the idea of a nation loosing its Empire wholesale and at the same time devoting itself to budgerigars, but the thought reminds me sharply of the Roman decadence when any amusement sufficed, provided its charms were sufficiently fleeting. I like the notice displayed in the window, 'Engraving can be arranged here'. There is a formal quality about the 'arranged', a politeness implying a refusal to rush things. Architecturally, Leadenhall Market is one of the many Victorian variants of neo-Classic, the style that the nineteenth-century architects picked out of the breakdown of tradition; not monumental Classic, like St. George's Hall, Liverpool, simply Victorian Market Classic, with trimmings.

London's great achievement in cast iron was, of course, the Crystal Palace, of which nothing now remains but windswept steps on which the grass grows and a few decaying bits of sculpture. But part of this fairy palace remains still in Kensington Gardens—the Coalbrookdale Gate. This is worth inspection as an example of the style, ornately decorative, which characterized the Great Exhibition. Originally the gates stood inside the Crystal Palace, but were re-erected half a mile away when the Exhibition was over at the entrance to Kensington Gardens. Incidentally, the site of the Crystal Palace can still be made out. There is a long stretch of grass in Hyde Park, in line with the Albert Memorial; looking towards the memorial, that is towards Kensington, a decrepit tree can be seen, protected by railings. This is supposed to be the last survivor of the elms which were enclosed in Paxton's glass palace. At any rate, this stretch of parkland is the site of the 1851 Exhibition. The Crystal Palace, although Paxton's masterpiece, and one of the most remarkable buildings of its time (remaining to this day one of the most satisfactory attempts at prefabrication) was not exactly unique, except in purpose and scale. It had been preceded by his own conservatory at Chatsworth, Burton's Palm House at Kew and Loudon, the successful landscape gardener and author/architect had published years before ideas for similar but smaller constructions. One of the prettiest buildings of this kind in London is the Floral Hall, Covent Garden, somewhat resembling a miniature Crystal Palace; it was originally an annexe of the Opera House.

There are two or three other kinds of street furnishings in metal which, alone or in combination, would make an interesting tour of London. I refer to the cast-iron balconies, an essential ingredient in the design of terraces of all grades throughout London, and the statues and drinking fountains or conduits. Many of the last—to take them first—are the minor pleasantries of London. There is the very Victorian drinking fountain at Gloucester Gate, Regent's Park, a pile of picturesquely arranged rocks from the top of which a mid-Victorian girl, hand shading her eyes, gazes over Camden Town, as if on some lee shore, scanning the horizon in search of a homeward-bound Indiaman. On a rock below is a cluster of brass leaves with a button in the centre, marked 'Push'. Those solid rocks are faced with brick at the back, which, if you peer behind, rather destroys the illusion. Last time I passed it, however, the period flavour was very evident; I was driving in a dog cart with Mr. Walter Gilbey just after the Easter horse parade, and in front of the statue were other little carts, fat ponies, donkeys, men in bowler hats, girls with coloured umbrellas—a perfect subject for Tissot. There are many other drinking fountains in London, many of them of small proportions, such as the one which gives such a charming touch to the church of St. Dunstan in the West, Fleet Street, The Edwardian one with a scallop shell canopy in Kensington High Street, the old water conduit by the Royal Exchange on Cornhill, Aldgate Pump and many others worth seeing, such as the remains of the old well in Well Walk, a relic of the days when Hampstead had aspirations to become a second Tunbridge Wells. With these, I might group the interesting parish boundary marks of London, sometimes sculptured but usually in cast iron. There are many parishes in the City alone (though the number of City churches has been dwindling since the Fire), and each parish was very jealous of its boundaries, hence the boundary marks fixed to houses and other buildings. Quite a few, such as those in the parish of St. Martin-in-the-Fields, had a device or badge, and others contented themselves with lettering and the date. From this, the expression 'out of bounds' undoubtedly originates, the parish bounds being beaten at Rogationtide.

To a rapid round-up of such curiosities, we can add the interest that lies in the search for sculptured signs and plaques, for instance, the sculptured badges of the Inns of Court, such as the Agnus Dei which appears on the buildings of the Middle Temple, and the winged horse, the griffin and lion of the others. In similar vein is the popinjay carved on the front of a building in Fleet Street, with the history of a monastic foundation behind it. This is Ulster House, 112, Fleet Street, now the London office of the *Belfast Telegraph*. Besides the carved popinjay swinging in his hoop is a tablet recording that the Inn of the Abbots of Cirencester stood here in the fifteenth century. The abbots stayed here when matters of state or religion made their presence in London necessary, and the Popinjay Inn, whose sign

Landscape at the Angel

is one of the oldest in Fleet Street, had a spacious garden running as far back as Harp Alley, commemorated in the present day 'Poppins Court', which is immediately east of Ulster House. So much of interest can lie behind a sign. . . .

London has much small scale ironwork, ranging from the simple but elegant railings of King's Bench Walk to those majestic ones of St. Paul's, or from the charming glazed passages of the houses on Cheyne Walk to magnificent iron gates like those in front of the College of Heralds, but perhaps the ironwork of the terraced houses is most unique and most undervalued. As I have said, it can be found all over London, even on the poorer terraces. This delicate ironwork gives the right foil to the studied simplicity of the façades. Even the dullest work of the third-rate architects and ordinary builders is usually redeemed by these balcony railings, often a pleasing contrast being formed by the use of Gothic balcony railings on the façade of a terrace of standard nineteenth-century type. L. N. Cottingham, who appears for a moment in the chapter on Gothic London, was one of the architects to issue pattern books of designs for window-guards and railings. Cottingham, besides being a Gothicist, provided much terraced housing of a competent but uninspired kind in South-west London. His balcony designs, however, sometimes reminiscent of Soane or Adam, often in the 'Grecian taste' are charming and effective. After Waterloo, the London balcony was often the only concession to decoration, a purpose it fulfils even when it becomes severely reduced to nothing more than vertical members joined by a couple of connecting rails or, slightly less severe, panels filled with lozenges formed by the intersection of diagonals. Such balconies give character to the great squares of Bloomsbury and variety to many of the shabby terraces of the vast areas east of Aldgate. They are as characteristic of London as the circular coal-hole cover of the pavements.

6

London Gothic

As my concern in this book is solely with the more neglected, less appreciated aspects of London, 'Gothic' in this chapter is that of the nineteenth-century middle ages. Medieval architecture proper, of which London has many examples, has been adequately dealt with elsewhere. I have already discussed one or two Gothic Revival buildings, notably St. Pancras Station, one of the many surviving in all parts of London. Only in comparatively recent years has the architecture of the Gothic Revival received the appreciation it merits, and with it the Victorian age itself, a period hard to get into focus. The conflicting currents of ideas, taste and attitudes fundamental to the nature of the age give it a Proteus-like character not easy to identify with exactness. All ages are ages of transition, but the Victorian era was more radical than most and much of its achievement was experimental or tentative. This many-sided character is, of course, one of the secrets of its fascination. We are in turn appalled by the social conditions (though at the present time we have become over-touchy and solicitous in such matters), impressed by the work of the engineers and engineer architects and we wonder at the apparent contradictions between the romantic spirit of the age and its utilitarianism, to say no more. It is not my intention to unravel all these varied threads, as, to paraphrase Pater, we ought to be too busy seeing and touching to theorize on what we see and touch: one thing is certain and that is the Victorian age, especially in the fifties and sixties, was capable of the highest romantic art. The Pre-Raphaelite movement is a sufficient proof of that. Their paintings—such as 'Autumn Leaves', 'April Love' and the 'English Autumn Afternoon'—certain poems by Morris and Patmore and the illustrators of the sixties lead us into an enchanted world, possessing a curious half-melancholy power over the mind. This was one aspect, and the most important, of nineteenth-century romanticism; another was the Gothic Revival. It is odd that the Pre-Raphaelites had little interest in contemporary Gothic;

68

in general they considered it mere copyism or servility. But the Gothic movement produced some highly original work in the hands of such men as Street and Butterfield, and it is easier now at this distance in time to appreciate the genuine romantic strains in nineteenth-century medievalism. Sometimes one can feel it in a sudden rush. I have often felt it myself, looking deep into the period and experiencing its Gothic fervour, when studying such churches as Butterfield's All Saints in Margaret Street near the B.B.C. Such occasions, poignant and intensely vivid, have a way, momentarily, of eradicating the passage of time.

I don't propose to burden the general reader with a history of the Gothic Revival, but it is necessary to have a little knowledge of it in order to enjoy it properly. It has a complex history, but can be briefly stated as a part of the wider romantic movement which spread over Europe in the nineteenth century, having its beginnings before the classically inspired period of Wincklemann and Goethe had lost its momentum. Romantic art is at any time a possibility in England; therefore one cannot say where the period ends; it is always latent! Liverpool Cathedral, still under construction, is Gothic Revival, but the fire has gone out of it; imposing at a distance, it is cold, hard and formal. Like Esperanto, it betrays no enthusiasm, no accidents, no history. For size and general scale, Liverpool Cathedral might be compared with the earliest large-scale use of revived Gothic, the Houses of Parliament. (Lovers of London, especially Gothic London, can congratulate themselves that the Parliament buildings were built at this mid-way period of the revival; the later more correct but academic Gothic of Sir Gilbert Scott would have been disastrous in Westminster.) Where Liverpool is dry and calculating, the Palace of Westminster, every inch of which was designed by Pugin (Barry was responsible for the plan and general arrangements) reflects the fervour and enthusiasm of a Gothic fanatic, which is what Pugin was. This gives life and authenticity to the carved work, overcoming to a large extent the lack of Gothic experience of the masons employed.

Earlier still, and one of the most successful buildings of the Gothic Revival, is St. Luke's, Chelsea, where Dickens was married. It is the very essence of the early revival, and was designed by John Savage in 1819 and completed in 1824. It was one of a number built by the Government under the Church Building Act for the rapidly growing districts. Since Classic styles were still employed, particularly those of the Greek Revival, many of the churches built under the act were at least Classic in intention. Several, such as St. John's, Waterloo Road, have distinct architectural qualities. But Gothic architecture, being little understood, produced some weird churches in London and the provinces; 'Commissioners' Gothic' the

Stones of Westminster: St. James the Less

style came to be called. Nearly all were so utilitarian as to be eminently unromantic, but I have in general a liking for them, especially when, furred with soot in the north of England, they tower over a manufacturing town, over the chip and tripe shops and pigeon-haunted backyards. Such Gothic fancies deserve greater study than has been given to them. St. Luke's, Chelsea, is a notable design and of unusually solid construction for the period. It is an exciting design, and one much enhanced by the honey-coloured stone employed which has weathered to exactly the right condition. The afternoon sun, picking out the flying buttresses from a brown shadow, highlights the panelled tower all the way up, creating an impression like that of a nineteenth-century steel engraving. This effect is aided by the spacious setting with well grown trees in the wide churchyard garden. Savage gave the church a fine interior, with slender clustered stone columns (these were often of cast iron at this date), a stone vaulted roof, possibly the earliest of the revival, and a triforium and clerestory. But it is the exterior with its slender, dramatic tower that catches our imagination—it is, in fact, magnificent scenery, and scenic qualities are an essential ingredient in all architecture worth the name. Incidentally, there is a tunnel in Britten Street, close to St. Luke's, running from the church to the Builders Arms, built at the same time as the church to serve the thirsty workmen.

My drawing of the offices in Eastcheap bring me to another aspect of London Gothic—the medieval offices of the sixties and seventies. Many still remain in such streets as Queen Victoria Street, and there is that splendid building in Lothbury, now occupied by an insurance company, but once the Bank of Australasia, that is a realization in stone of the writings of Ruskin and Street: the *Stones of Venice* brought to the City. I recommend a visit to it to enjoy its useless, elaborately pierced balconies, its inset panels of marble, Venetian arches and polychrome decoration; the more so, as in juxtaposition with Wren's St. Margaret's Church and Soane's part of the Bank of England, it gives one food for thought in the matter of varying architectural tastes. These Gothic offices are gradually disappearing; more is the pity. Recalling all the directors' offices I have been in, I cannot recall one that was not dull and unimaginative. Company directors either go for something nearly up to date (but not quite) or else, having a tendency to good taste, make a set at Regency or stockbrokers' Chippendale. My office would be different. It would be Gothic-Morris-Beardsley. For preference, I should select offices in one of the earliest and gloomiest Gothic blocks I could find. If a dog cart were unsuitable, I should drive up in a vintage motor, and the chauffeur would have a tightly buttoned coat, leggings and goggles. My own coat would be of fur, quite splendid and of incredible weight, and when not in use, would have its own seat in the back of the motor. Visitors would pass through my secretary's room, the walls of which would be hung with William Morris paper—a late one—acanthus on dark blue. The telephone and typewriter would be of the period, and so would the girl, whose terms of employment would include wearing high-necked blouses, long skirts and black shoes with buckles. Sometimes she would appear in button boots or occasionally in a Pre-Raphaelite dress of willowy green, like a Walter Crane drawing. On a side table would be slender copies of Baudelaire and Rossetti and leather-bound volumes of *The Savoy* and *The House of Pomegranates*. In my own office, I should offer Turkish cigarettes and hock and seltzer, and the pottery would be by William de Morgan. On the walls, otherwise ostentatiously plain, would be drawings by Beardsley to astonish and delight my clients and guests. They would be drawings in which sinister women would smile in a rueful, aphrodisiacal manner, hungry for the next sensation but one, and there would be drawings by Rossetti, early watercolours bright like a medieval missal, Ruskins and a letter from Wilde to Bosie. . . .

The Eastcheap Gothic offices belong to the style developed in the late 1850's and throughout the '60's. It is fantastic Victorian Gothic at its most assured, highly complex and with a profusion of curiously intersecting planes, canopies, columns and window-openings. It is surface or street Gothic of a kind the Victorians hoped to develop, but they lacked models, at least English models, for most street architecture of the Middle Ages has disappeared. The nineteenth-century version illustrated here is highly competent, despite its restless, geometric vitality. As can be seen, the high Victorian Gothic manner is fully developed here, hardly a surface without ornament. The influence of Ruskin and Street can be found in it, but its elements consist largely of motifs taken from French and Italian Gothic, fused in the Sir Gilbert Scott manner to form the fully developed Victorian style which can never be mistaken for any other. It is worth going to East-cheap to see it, for London, unlike Manchester, is not so well equipped with Gothic offices and the material (brick, coloured brick, stone, tile and ironwork) is like the Lothbury office, the Gothic word made flesh. It forms a piquant contrast to Wren's church of St. Margaret Pattens and the old-fashioned and delightful shop adjoining it.

There are a few Gothic warehouses left in London. Red Lion Wharf on Bankside, dating from 1865, is in red and blue brick, the blue being used to outline arches and also to form diaper patterns on the wall surfaces, and a few Gothic warehouses remain in Upper Thames Street. Charles L. East-lake's book, *A History of the Gothic Revival*, Longmans, Green (London, 1872), is an invaluable guide to London Gothic, for many of the buildings

Eastcheap Gothic

described still exist in a more or less complete form. In these pages, the Gothic ideals and aspirations of that time (the happiest, possibly, for a leisured Englishman that has ever been known) stir once again, so that one feels impelled to rush out to relish all the Victorian Gothic that can be seen. This very strong flavour of mid-century Gothic can be sensed in several of the London churches, particularly, I think, in St. James the Less in Thorndike Street off the Vauxhall Bridge Road which I illustrated on page 70. I cannot do better than quote Eastlake's description of it at length. After referring to the infiltration of a French element into the Gothic of this period, he says:

'But in no instance was this revolt from national style more marked than in the Church of St. James the Less, erected at Westminster by Mr. Street. Here the whole character of the building, whether we regard its plan, its distinctive features, its external or internal decoration is eminently un-English. Even the materials used in its construction and the mode by which it is lighted were novelties. The detached tower with its picturesquely modelled spire, its belfry stage rich in ornamental brickwork and marble bosses, the semicircular apse and quasi-transepts, the plate tracery, the dormers inserted in the clerestory, the quaint treatment of the nave arcade, the bold vigour of the carving, the chromatic decoration of the roof—all bear evidence of a thirst for change which Mr. Street could satisfy without danger, but which betrayed many of his contemporaries into intemperance. Even here there is something to regret in the restless notching of edges, the dazzling distribution of stripes, the multiplicity of pattern forms, and exuberance of sculpture detail. But it is all so clever and so facile, so evidently the invention of a man who enjoys his work—and who, full of rich fancies and quaint conceits, is incapable of insipidity, but at any moment if he so chooses can rein himself back from extravagance—that it is impossible but to regard it with pleasure.

'If Mr. Street had never designed anything but the campanile of this church—and its Italian character justifies the name—it would be sufficient to proclaim him an artist. In form, proportion of parts, decorative detail, and in use of colour, it seems to leave little to be desired. To form a just appreciation of its merits, let the architectural amateur walk down to Garden Street from any part of London, and note as he passes the stereotyped patterns of towers and spires which he will find to right or left of his road. How neat, how respectable, how correct, how eminently uninteresting they are! No one cares to look at them twice. They are all like each other, or so little different that if they changed places any day, by help of Aladdin's lamp, the London world would never find it out. But here, in one of the poorest and meanest quarters of town, hidden away behind dull masses of brick and mortar, this fair tower, when one does see it, is something not to be easily forgotten.'

Street, who was assuredly a master of style, repeated this success a few years later at the end of the 1860's with his church of St. Mary Magdalene in Woodchester Street, Paddington, this time with a dramatic octagonal spire, horizontally striped at the belfry stage—a sort of fusion of Lombardic and German Gothic elements. Both these churches were highly ritualistic: church and pub alike supplied warmth and colour in these drab London districts.

Entering St. James the Less is like walking into a Victorian chromolithograph. The interior is a profusion of gilding, brick, tile and marble. Almost every surface is carved or decorated, and must be savoured slowly, like old claret. The coloured decoration—in fact the whole interior—has become more harmonious with the passage of time. There is a superb metal canopy over the font and (wonderfully Victorian) the illuminated words 'Flower Fund' in an Oxford frame. The church gives an overwhelming, intense feeling of the 1860's—crinolined, bonneted figures would not be in the least surprising, for in entering the church one has left behind the world of sliced super loaves and electrically propelled milkmen. Phrases from the *Stones of Venice* or Street's own book spring to mind all the time. There is a Christ in Glory faded and peeling above the chancel arch. What did the Victorian working classes think of it all? One can only guess and return to the world outside where the sunlight casts detailed shadows, like those in a Ruskin drawing done long ago in Verona, on the London pavement and on the kids playing by the magnificent corroding Gothic railings.

The Baroness Burdett Coutts, who appears later in this chapter in connection with her work in Bethnal Green, was one of the many architectural patrons who favoured Gothic. In the middle of the century, parts of Westminster were distinctly slum, among them Vincent Square. Here she built St. Stephen's Church, designed by Benjamin Ferry in 1846. In this case, the style was 'Decorated', and though the building has turned black in the London atmosphere, it is a good example of the kind of Gothic which was to become de rigeur—except in the case of the work of outstanding men like Butterfield, knowledgeable but dull. Butterfield's church of All Saints, Margaret Street, must be visited by those in search of London Gothic. Grouped round a small courtyard entered by an iron gate, the composition announces itself as the product of an original, wayward mind, and at the same time has upon it the strange period flavour of The Seven Lamps of Architecture, with strongly Puseyite overtones. As with Butterfield's church of St. Alban, Holborn (recently restored after war damage),

The last of the Columbia Market

All Saints was also in a poor district: High Church theology and the architecture of ritualism, all marble, mosaic and pattern seems to have been offered as a specific in many rundown Metropolitan areas—a sublimated version, perhaps, of the Victorian custom of pouring soup into elderly, indigent widows.

Probably the exterior of All Saints, with its soaring, green slated spire, is the most satisfactory part of the design. The brick houses attached to the church are worth study as they anticipate William Morris's and Webb's ideas, carried out much later at the Red house, Bexley Heath. Inside, the wealth and variety of materials employed give an almost Byzantine colour effect, and it is all so wonderfully shiny, a characteristic never known in previous Gothic periods. The columns in the Nave arcade of Aberdeen granite have richly carved capitals of alabaster, and an elaborate pattern fills in the spaces of the arch spandrils above. In fact the interior of the church has hardly an area left undecorated. To visit All Saints and then to step outside into the present-day London of the surrounding streets is to experience a curiously contradictory sensation, as the church seems to exist in another dimension of time altogether.

The churches mentioned above are but a few of the many examples of nineteenth-century Victorian Gothic in London. To them I add a few others as the basis of a romantic tour: St. Mary Magdalene, Bermondsey (an entirely delightful 'tea garden' Gothic tower of about 1830 in stucco); Holy Trinity, Sloane Street (1880–90), late Gothic Revival, a highly personal Gothic crossed with a trace of *art nouveau* elements and a Morris-inspired Arts and Crafts flavour thrown in, by Sedding; St. Stephen, Hampstead, by S. S. Teulon in 1869, coloured brick, apsidal chancel, central tower, French Gothic of a peculiarly unwieldy kind, very period; Catholic Apostolic Church, Gordon Square, Bloomsbury, next to University College, on a cathedral scale, 1851–5, by R. Brandon, spire never completed. Islington has a few churches by Barry. Perhaps the best is Holy Trinity in Cloudesley Square, 1826. Lastly, St. Augustine, Kilburn, High Victorian Gothic, 1870–80, very solid and convincing, by Pearson.

London possesses a rich supply of Gothic villas of the sort that have been christened 'Wimbledon Gothic'. These villas naturally occur in all those areas of London built up by the Victorians—Norwood and Wimbledon, for instance. Some of them are in a pleasing state of decay. They were originally villas built for the newly prosperous middle class, with Gothic ideas taken, very unfeelingly, from the writings of Ruskin—Venetian windows, slippery porches of encaustic tile and, what distressed Ruskin most of all, striped and banded brickwork, the streaky bacon style. With these may be grouped those villas with a surface of Gothic, that is a fashion-

The romance of Bethnal Green: Columbia Square

able front tacked on to a house of normal London character. Two of these can be found in Westbridge Road, Battersea, a pair of semi-detached villas with a façade of flint and stone. Each house has a statue in a canopied niche in the gable, and the style is that of the late 1830's or early 1840's. Gothic tracery appears in the windows on the ground floor, and the porches have narrow Gothic panels. Quite characteristically, the backs of these houses are built of London stockbrick and have sash windows of the common type. This is toy Gothic, of which the best domestic example in London is perhaps Hunters Lodge, Hampstead, dating from 1825, in the ornamental cottage style. St. John's Wood is, of all London districts, the one offering most in the way of toy or ornamental Gothic. It was the first part of London to be developed in this way, i.e. with detached and semi-detached houses, and when the building rush started in 1820–30, the district was quickly built up. To this rapid building up in the early Victorian period, the district owes its special quality. The Woronzow Almshouses of mid-1830's Tudor are worth seeing, as are most almshouses of this date. With these can be grouped the two Park Villages begun by Nash in 1824, designed as a sort of suburban picturesque village. These two model villages are in a variety of styles as well as stuccoed Tudor or Gothic.

Lastly, for Late Victorian Gothic, I would recommend the Tower House in Melbury Road, Kensington, in which the fittings, cupboards, fireplaces and so on have been preserved as they were left by the architect, W. Burges, who built the house for his own occupation. Autumn is the time to see it, when, mysterious in the dusk, its stained glass windows glimmer with a faint light from out of the Virginia creeper mantling the conical tower in red, gold and amber. Only passers-by and cars break up the period illusion and harmony created by the architecture, the darkness and the falling leaves.

The double page drawing on p. 78 is of one of the most unbelievable sights in London, of a Gothic dreariness almost impossible to describe, the working-class dwellings in Columbia Square, Bethnal Green. These blocks were built by Baroness Burdett-Coutts. They were designed by Darbishire, who also produced some for the Peabody Trust. Columbia Square must have been depressing when new; today it is of appallingly melancholy aspect. In this huge open space, the sun seems to burn up the yellowing grass and ragwort. The sun's rays are reflected back from the innumerable pieces of broken glass, and the square is deserted and silent apart from a few dead-end kids and the chimes of the choc-ice man. These tenements are now almost empty. Windows are gaping and sightless and the wooden Gothic pinnacles of the attic storey are decaying and broken —like the monument in the centre of my drawing. Columbia Square is

Waterloo Road Gothic

like a Gothic barracks, a sort of nightmare caricature of *The Stones of Venice*. On the monument can be read

Columbia Square
Built by Angela Georgina Burdett Coutts
East
Commenced May 1858
Completed May 1859
It is 176 feet long   32 feet wide   55 feet high
It contains 52 Tenements or 116 Rooms

81

There are similar inscriptions for other sides and the half obliterated motto, 'As every thread of Gold is valuable So is every minute of Time'.

Next to the Square, on what is now a great empty site, Baroness Burdett Coutts built the vast market hall, the Columbia Market. I wish I had recorded it for this book before demolition, as it was quite unique. No verbal description could convey the strangeness and unlikelihood of it all— that great place like a medieval cloth hall, with a gatehouse and cloisters. The building (also by H. A. Darbishire) belonged to the late 1860's, and had a tall tower; the interior was a mass of tall piers, vaults and tracery, and full of carved inscriptions. Like Fonthill Abbey, nothing is left but a pile of rubble and its loss to London was incalculable. Only a few pillars and a little ironwork remains here and there, and this I have drawn on p. 76.

For the frontispiece to this book, I have drawn one of the queerest Gothic houses in London. This is in St. John's Wood, but much later than those already mentioned. The house is to be found in Langford Place, and is worth drawing and describing if only for a strange atmosphere which can be felt very readily. How it acquired its ghostly quality, I am unable to say—but that bay window, was there ever anything quite like it? It seems to come forward in menacing fashion, like a great helmet, and the tracery below is filled with stained glass of lilies. Even on a day of light and summer sun, this window has a sinister air about it, untoward and oppressive as if possessed of some fearful secret. The room behind it has an uncanny atmosphere, not precisely ghostly but, just as in the garden, *you feel you are being watched*. Certainly, this is the place to read Harrison Ainsworth and all the ghostly books ever written.

To end this chapter on a lighter note, I have illustrated an oddity from the site of the new traffic roundabout in Waterloo Road. The Gothic arch, a genuine one, was below the premises occupied by a pawnbroker. Years ago, the house was occupied by an architect I have already mentioned— L. N. Cottingham, designer of terraces and iron balconies. Cottingham was extensively employed as a 'restorer' of old churches, and from these restorations, he assembled a rich collection of carving in wood and stone, stained glass and other church fittings, which ought, of course, to have been left intact. No doubt, all these restorer's relics will be swept away long before this book is published.

7

The Mysterious East

including Bermondsey and Deptford

Eᴀꜱᴛ ᴏꜰ St. Paul's lies a huge area offering much of interest to the London perambulator. Parts of the East End, especially Limehouse, have already been discussed; they are, however, only a few of the East End parishes where discoveries are to be made, in tours taking in such places as Wapping, Bethnal Green, Spitalfields and the Whitechapel and Commercial Roads. One can start at Stepney Green Underground Station, close to Charrington's Brewery. Here in Stepney Green are a few old houses remaining from what, in the eighteenth century, must have been a quiet village green. The old houses have been allowed to decay and shops are built out in front on the usual London system, but there are the remains of carved and pedimented doorways here and there. These and the old almshouses give some indication of the quality of the place before it decayed. There is at least one house with a hooded, shell-patterned porch and some bits of rather good ironwork. The almshouses, originally built by the Corporation of Trinity House, were for 'decayed masters and commanders of ships or the widows of such', and were built in 1695. The almshouses have been successfully restored after war damage. But more unusual is the pretty little Bellevue Place, illustrated on page 93. Bellevue Place is off Stepney Green, down a little street by the side of the brewery. A green gate opening in the wall leads to a totally unexpected corner of London, one that may well disappear if Charrington's, who own the property, ever decide to expand. Bellevue Place is well named. It is a cul-de-sac with a paved pathway leading to the far end, under a creeper-covered wall. The cottages are early nineteenth century, and have true cottage gardens fenced with wooden rails, pointed at the top. Here are unbelievably rural gardens, full of lilac, roses, hydrangeas, wallflowers, lupins and delphiniums—all a minute's walk from the Mile End Road.

From here you turn in the direction of the City and the Whitechapel Road. Above the cafés, cheap dress shops, and gents' outfitters are the

83

remains of old terraced houses, but to get the feeling of Whitechapel, it is necessary to leave the main road and plunge into the maze of streets behind —the London of Jack the Ripper and a man of quite another calibre, General Booth. Streets such as Greatorex Street and Montague Street give off the full Whitechapel flavour. Montague Street is particularly rich in tottering old property and greasy doorways. There are an astonishing number of cast-iron posts dotted about—one every few feet in places— the tops of which have a patina created by the polish of innumerable elbows. This is the place to study the Jewish butchers and poulterers, often established in crazy old shops. With these go the small one-man tailoring businesses and barbers, nearly all with foreign names above the door. Small, close-smelling shops sell Jewish candlesticks, Old Testaments, the Talmud, the Psalms of David and Songs of Zion. An entire alley opposite the Whitechapel Bell Foundry supports itself by the sale of Hebrew lucky charms and cheap gaudy jewellery. This part of Whitechapel abounds with shops for the sale of oily fish and crummy little eating-places. Above the shops, the property is invariably in an advanced state of decay; old enamel advertisements assist in keeping the powdery brickwork together.

In the Whitechapel Road once again, the East London Art Gallery (Townsend, 1897–9) is a curious, indigestible *art nouveau* design, and must have appeared very revolutionary when new. Next comes Spitalfields, an area of fine decaying Georgian architecture, some wonderfully grim blocks of Peabody Buildings and other 'Improved dwellings for the Poor'. Spital- fields collapsed suddenly in the nineteenth century as a place of residence, and the fine houses were turned into tenements, before that, however, the district was considered eligible by such men as Bolingbroke. Elder Street is full of fine ironwork and doorways, and there is an extensive collection in other streets—Fournier Street, Folgate Street, for example—mostly early eighteenth century. In Spital Square is the exceptionally good bonded warehouse of Sadler and Moore. The rain-water heads, gauged brick cornices and ornamental iron railings are still intact. The door of No. 20 (Bolingbroke's house) was altered to the present one in the Bedford Square style. It has delicate Adamesque features, and the rusticated quoins and keystones are carried out in Coade's artificial stone. The earlier eighteenth- century windows can be seen above. One of the finest eighteenth-century shops in the whole of London is here, in Artillery Lane. However, as this is well known, I have chosen to illustrate a curiosity instead—the Moorish bazaar in Fashion Street, given an odd realism by the turbaned figures of Indians who have drifted into the area. It was once the Jews' market, a place for the sale of cheap textiles, penny notebooks and fifty-bladed penknives. Buildings with a Turkish or Moorish touch invariably appeal to me, by their utter disregard of architectural qualities. I have a liking for the tawdry, extravagant and eccentric, and appreciate the whimsical logic involved in making a Turkish baths a place of onion domes and minarets. It was not the Turks who invented the bath named after them, by the way; in fact, we owe it to the Greeks and Romans. Not many Turkish delights survive in London, but there is a curious Moorish bit at the foot of Black-friars Bridge, carried out in stock brick. Seeking an Oriental mood, one has to visit Lord Leighton's house in Kensington to obtain the proper sur-roundings, apart from the mosques and synagogues. Next to Fashion Street is the strangely named Flower and Dean Street, one of the worst areas in London in the mid-nineteenth century and later close to the scene of the Jack the Ripper operations. This street is full of drab nineteenth-century flats busting at the seams with life, both human and animal.

Jack the Ripper brings me to that other East End area of wonderful fascination—that of the Siege of Sidney Street and the anarchists. Half a century ago, the East End remained a closed book to the rest of London; hence the alarm created by the Houndsditch Murders and the ensuing gun battle of Sidney Street. Londoners realized the unpleasant fact that there were gunmen in their midst and a vast floating population of refugees and anarchists living somewhere or other only a short distance from the opulent City. Peter the Painter, that elusive, unsatisfactory figure, and his gun-toting friends have always fascinated me, and I have visited the scene of their operations time and again. Whenever I go, in spite of modern changes (though there is a great deal left unchanged), I seem to see the top-hatted figure of Winston Churchill peering round a doorway during the gun battle, and policemen with walrus moustaches stare out of the past, along with loungers in greasy cloth caps. If you go to Whitechapel today on a dark winter evening, it is easy to see how, in a part of London then lit with gas, and not too much of that, the Houndsditch murderers made their getaway. At that time, butchers, greengrocers and grocers, whose shops were open to the street, had their stock pinched before their eyes by experts in the art of disappearing into the shadows. Sidney Street is more orderly today, and on the site of the siege the houses have been replaced by flats, but I remember the besieged house clearly, part of a block which, at the time of the siege, housed poor working-class families, many of Jewish origin. I remember also a local coming out to watch me draw the house and telling me how he had watched the siege and the smoke coming out of the roof. It is quite incredible how many people round Sidney Street do remember the siege and the smoke coming out of the roof. On the opposite side to the new flats, however, the long row of two-storeyed terraced houses remain intact. They are of the usual East End type of yellow stock brick, and these certainly witnessed the affair. A modern note is struck by the doors, which are now painted, Chelsea fashion, in yellows, greens and blues.

The anarchists, two of whom perished in the Sidney Street siege, had their club in Jubilee Street. In this street lodged Leon Beron, murdered on Clapham Common, 1911, and so this near slum street (the anarchists were as poverty-stricken as everyone else in the district in 1911) forms a link between Sidney Street, the Clapham affair and the shootings in Houndsditch. Unfortunately, the anarchists' club has gone, but my drawing shows the street looking exactly as it did when it was the centre of the activity for those shadowy figures, Beron, Steinie Morrison and the rest. Jubilee Street, E.1, has houses of a better type than those of Sidney Street, and there are some good ornamental balconies which help to break up the monotony. Above the line of the cornice is a perspective of disproportionate chimney pots, a characteristic feature of the old London working-class streets. In the centre of the drawing is a dairy, obviously early nineteenth century, with thin wooden pilasters and a deep cornice. The street forms a dimly classically inspired background to the largely unsolved crimes, but the anarchists, following the example of their club have disappeared from view, along with the furtive loafers and other flotsam and jetsam, and have been replaced by cars, mopeds and prosperous-looking families.

Ashfield Street, round the corner, has a terrace of decaying houses with 'Tudor' dripstones over the ground floor windows, a desolate feature not improved by decaying stucco streaked with yellow and black. Some of the windows still have their original shutters; a surprising number of these still remain in the East End. Turning westwards again and on the Whitechapel Road, the market in Hessel Street is worth inspection for its pronounced Yiddish flavour. Most of the street and the stalls comprise Kosher butchers, poulterers and fish shops, well patronized by the Hagars and Ishmaels of Whitechapel. This brings me to the illustration of the Grand Palais on page 101. Today the Grand Palais is given over to the thrills of Bingo, but was until a few years ago a Yiddish music-hall. The interior is rather interesting, small and compact—no elaborate decoration—in fact, it has the atmosphere of a small provincial concert hall. Only the initiated could relish the Jewish music-hall turns; no one else could. The posters, however, were most decorative and almost entirely in Hebrew, printed in red and blue. It is a pity that such old style entertainments have faded out, as the Yiddish Theatre was unique in its way, but fortunately the building remains intact. When Aldgate is reached, the Hoop and Grapes and the adjoining house are too good to be missed. Very likely they date from before the Great Fire, and certainly represent the appearance of London houses at that period.

Shad Thames

'We sing in the streets because Jesus is our friend.' This scene takes place outside another building dedicated to Bingo, the former Palace Cinema in Deptford, the time being Saturday morning, the best time to visit this interesting and picturesque locality. The announcement is made by one of the intrepid ladies of the Salvation Army, shouting through a megaphone. I greatly admire the Salvation Army, not only because it takes courage to stand up for one's convictions in public, but also because they accept so much of London's dirty work. Whether they know it or not, the Salvation Army is very period, exceptionally so. I hope they will always retain those unbecoming coalscuttle poke bonnets. 'Yes, Jesus is our friend', repeats the megaphone, and I look round at the audience, awaiting the Bingo session. They are a curious, listless group to watch—these Guys and Dolls. The females of the species are just as deadly as the male, if anything slightly more in need of a wash, and roll their marble eyes disdainfully over the healthy Salvation Army warriors. ('We'll cling to the old rugged Cross,' continues the megaphone, 'and exchange it some day for a crown.') Although no word is spoken, except by the tin trumpet, one feels that a chronic apathy exists . . . the teddy boys and louts in leather jackets nudge their fun-molls and chew their cud. Suddenly the atmosphere is electrified by a curious pantomime—a shrivelled-up white woman, red-eyed and as thin as a rake, is chased across the road by a great hulking brute of a negro, both screaming like mad. This is more than enough to divert the wandering attention of the Jean-agers, and the crowd, now forgetful alike of the Salvation Army and the Bingo, disappears.

A stone's throw away is the market in Douglas Way, a Hogarthian scene on Saturday. Vegetable stalls without number appear, stalls full of disinfectant and toilet paper and those selling lino and rugs. There are stalls selling pet foods, especially strong in budgie-toys, stalls of tinned fruit, wireless stalls. That almost obsolete form of transport, the horse and cart, comes into its own in Douglas Way, and very nice these carts sometimes are, too, decorated with curvy flourishes, fat roses and carving, here and there. It is like the London of Phil May, less vigorous, perhaps, but the jokes still have the special London quality. At the end of the street are junk dealers' stalls—pitches only, many of them—a pile of miscellaneous goods laid out on the pavement, but the junk and marine store dealers appear to be decreasing in numbers. Although I have made one or two finds in this market, including a complete set of old kitchen jars for four shillings, straight off the pavement, the wares have a dreary look about them. Battered suitcases minus a lock or the handle are nearly always found. Victorian sewing machines, also hardy perennials, fail to arouse a desire for possession, and there are impossible beady lampshades left over from the

Bermondsey Street

nineteen-twenties. Great shapeless masses of scrap iron erupt on the paving stones, together with decrepit television sets, old clothes, ancestors with mutton-chop whiskers and other articles whose specific purpose, if they ever possessed such, can now only be guessed.

Deptford High Street is crossed by a rather interesting bridge, carrying the Greenwich Railway. The bridge is supported on Doric columns of cast iron, and dates from the late 1830's. Saturday morning is the time to see the human element at its richest in Deptford, and in the crowded High Street are all sorts of buskers and street entertainers whose presence gives additional character to the street: an organ grinder, perhaps, whose instrument is more properly termed 'a street piano' (there is still one firm left hiring out the 'pianos' in London, near Saffron Hill: look for the pictures of Edwardian beauties on the panels of the organ), one-man bands, sellers of *Old Moore's Almanack* and so on. Today, a couple of stocky, red-faced men take their stand under the railway bridge—one plays an accordion and the other sings 'The Mountains of Mourne'. Appropriately, too, for Irish ideas are not lacking in Deptford—witness the large pub charmingly named The Harp of Erin and here today at the Catholic Church a gaudy Irish wedding takes place. As the bride and groom assemble on the steps, they are joined by their families and friends, the women in pale blue and the men in navy-blue suits. All wear large pink carnations, and the men's faces, each creased in a wide grin, are all red from the application of yellow soap. Small boys, also in blue suits and with even shinier faces, cross their legs uneasily, and the accordion plays 'The Meeting of the Waters'.

Off the High Street is one of the most remarkable streets in the East End of London, Albury Street, with its extensive collection of doorways, one of which is drawn on page 95. Both sides of the street have a succession of early eighteenth-century houses of two or three storeys. The architect is unknown, but almost identical houses occurred in Rotherhithe. The comparison can no longer be made, as the latter have now been demolished, but this similarity led me to think, especially in view of the carving (foliage, cherubs' heads and whole cherubs) that these houses were the homes of ships' captains and officers of standing, owners of ships perhaps, who had them built to their design, the carving being done by the ships' carvers of the district. There was a flourishing school of naval carvers at that period, largely located in Rotherhithe in the early eighteenth century. Why this street of fine houses should have been built here is otherwise a mystery, and it is certainly curious that the style of carving should so closely resemble the stylized carving on ships' figureheads: one of the figures holds a chart and another a pair of dividers. The interiors of the houses have a narrow entrance hall, panelled like most of the rooms on the ground floor, and have

90

an arch midway between the street door and the staircase. Many of these staircases are remarkably fine, with exquisitely designed mouldings to the handrail and turned balustrades, both spiral and circular. Albury Street is the only part of Deptford to retain this eighteenth-century quality; nearly all the rest has gone, except for the Baroque church of St. Paul. St. Paul's Church is behind Albury Street, and was designed by Thomas Archer, an assistant of Wren, and dates from 1712 to 1730. St. Paul's like the other, more famous one, has an air of authority and complete assurance about it. There are great staircases of a sort that might form a fitting background to a masque, huge pilasters and a semicircular portico with massive Tuscan columns contrasting with the delicacy and formality of the steeple. It has in full measure those scenic qualities which, as I have said, are the hallmark of great architecture, together with a subtle melancholy feeling difficult to describe.

From here, one can either go along the High Street—noting the remains of eighteenth- and early nineteenth-century houses above the carpet and wireless shops—to see the fantastic music-hall (no longer used for this purpose) in the Broadway, dating from 1899, or go on to Greenwich. Greenwich is now emerging from a period of comparative neglect by London visitors, the reason for its revival being, of course, the *Cutty Sark*. Still, Greenwich is not yet sufficiently explored architecturally. In a quick review, I should include the delightful junk shop selling Victoriana, so crowded that to move about the premises is an occupational hazard, in a late Regency setting in Spread Eagle Yard, the little old-fashioned shops such as the florists where they have bunches of flowers in big Victorian jugs and the Regency terraces by the market in College Approach. Looking down this street gives a vista like an old print, especially on evenings in the autumn when the sky is full of strongly illuminated cumulus clouds, a view terminated by the huge globes on the gates of Greenwich Hospital. There are one or two bow-windowed shops about here, somehow with a maritime flavour, more junk shops and an eel-pie emporium, all of which are worth inspection, and the well-proportioned terraces at the corner of Nelson Road.

In Deptford once again, one of the most interesting experiences in connexion with this book was my visit to the Royal Victoria Yard in its latter days—at least as a naval establishment, for the vast area is to become part of a redevelopment scheme, but much of the old architecture is to be preserved and will be accessible to the public. Deptford was the scene of Samuel Pepys's attempts to end corruption, to organize the Fleet for the wars against the Dutch. At one time, the victualling of the Navy was carried on from a site on Tower Hill, near where the Mint now stands. As this

91

became inadequate, the Navy acquired thirty-five acres of land from Sir John Evelyn in 1742, and it became the Deptford Victualling Yard until Queen Victoria paid a visit in 1858 and commanded it to be called 'The Royal Victoria Yard'. There is a rich collection of eighteenth- and nineteenth-century buildings, for example the old bakery. The ovens, set in great arches of brick, are of cast iron from the Regent's Canal Ironworks, and are dated 1855. The ovens were for baking hard tack biscuits, and were used until 1906 when bread was introduced into the Navy. The meal was ground in the yard. In those days, cattle were brought to Deptford from Ireland and slaughtered in the cattle yard, the meat being salted and stowed in casks to await issue. There was also a chocolate mill which produced the cocoa for the Navy, in use until the last war. Bully beef was tinned here, too, in the nineteenth century. The whole group, sugar stores, warehouses, bakery, rum store and Governor's quarters, is still basically a Georgian enclave with old trees and eighteenth-century terraces and a most interesting river walk by the rum store. 'The Terrace' is to remain Admiralty property; one side of it has a fine exterior staircase of cast iron. When I was there, the place was largely deserted. I pushed open the door of the walled garden attached to the Governor's house. Old-fashioned Paisley pinks, streaked purple and white, were in flower in the overgrown borders. The vine was setting its green grapes in the conservatory. Innumerable sparrows were twittering in the huge old mulberry, for the day was hot, and the whole garden, in fact, was full of the song of birds, thrushes and blackbirds, mostly, and a steady burbling of unseen pigeons. All this was against the background noise of bumping barges and wailing river boats coming from the waterfront only a few yards away. There is an indescribable feeling of old sea battles here—no wonder, after two hundred years of service to the Navy, a feeling that Nelson and the Nile, Cape St. Vincent and Trafalgar were only yesterday.

Leaving the Yard, you go down Windmill Lane, past the pre-fabs and by the waste land where disused railway lines lead to nowhere and kids play in abandoned baths and old sinks, over the Surrey Canal where all the exhausted soil is covered with the Indian yellow flowers of the ragwort and light parachutes detach themselves from the willow-herb and commence their invasion of Deptford backyards.

It was at Deptford that I once saw one of the most interesting of the remaining street entertainments of London—a pearly-suited pair, presumably man and wife, doing a sort of clog dance in the street to the accompaniment of a concertina. Such entertainments are worth watching in present-day London, for they are disappearing rapidly. This is unfortunate, for those who get their living off the streets are essential to character and

The rural East End: Bellvue Place, Stepney Green

interest. With them, we might group such vestigial remains of old customs and games as are still carried on by children, handed down in some mysterious manner. I do not mean, of course, such street games as marbles, hopscotch or knucklebones which, although ancient (particularly knucklebones), are more well known and still, to a certain extent, played. I mean such curious London survivals as 'Remember the Grotto' which I once had the luck to see in the East End—Bermondsey, I think. The grotto is, or was, a pile of shells, oyster shells in Victorian London when this delicacy was so cheap, together with a few leaves and bits of coloured glass heaped up to form a sort of arbour, with a candle inside. 'A Penny to see the Grotto' was a familiar sound in London streets up to the turn of the century. Quite possibly the grotto had originally some religious significance. Whip tops can still be bought in little shops in the East End, though the game seems to be in a decline, and hoops have all but disappeared, but street games involving chants (also mysteriously handed down from one generation to another) are still popular. When I lived in Rotherhithe, the local kids used to play an ancient ring game to these words:

> ' *The good ship sails from the alley alley O*
> *The alley alley O, the alley alley O*
> *The good ship sails from the alley alley O*
> *On the twentieth of September.*'

Curiously enough, this folk chant survives in Ireland, though there the ship is a 'big ship' which sails *through* not *from* the alley and the date is the fourteenth of December. I wondered if the song had originated in Rotherhithe and referred to the *Mayflower*, which was built there; if so, a slight inaccuracy had crept in as to dates, for the *Mayflower*, after leaving the Rotherhithe Yards, left Plymouth on September 6th, 1620.

Most of these pleasures have to be searched for, though they make rewarding discoveries. As regards street vendors, I think my most pleasing encounter was the old woman selling lavender whom I once saw in Holborn —a Phil May figure with basket and apron. Lavender sellers are now very rare, having gone like the muffin men previously mentioned and sellers of ginger beer and hot pies. But Cruikshank recorded a picturesque aspect of London life in the shape of the seller of pot plants from a cart pulled by a donkey. These men of the costermongering class used to ply their trade round the better-class neighbourhoods, and drew attention to their wares with the cry 'All-a-blowing, all-a-growing'. It is an interesting fact that a few of these vendors of pot plants still carry on the trade, usually from a pretty little painted cart, drawn by a pony. In shape the cart is somewhat

Albury Street, Deptford

similar to the coster's barrow, but with the addition of an H-shaped frame at the front; the reins pass over the centre bar. And I have got much pleasure from the man who sells plants from an ordinary hand barrow in and about the Strand. In addition to the usual green matting, favoured by costers and undertakers, he has a display of religious pictures and texts pinned to the sides of the barrow and propped up among the boxes of pansies and other bedding-out stuff, a perambulating sermon as it were. Street photographers are worth looking out for, not the smooth operators with miniature cameras stationed at various strategic points, but the old-fashioned ones with a large camera on a tripod, direct descendants of the Victorian street photographers. These photographs, produced on the spot, are supplied in a paper frame, and have a distinct tendency to fade. Pavement musicians are too well known to be included here, as are the vendors of popular art in the form of London souvenirs and postcards, but there are other curious entertainments occasionally seen which belong to a bygone London, such as the one-man band I once followed in Bloomsbury. A large drum was fastened to his back and below that a kettle drum, both being worked by an elaborate system of string. Cymbals were fixed to the man's legs and a perfect orchestra of wind instruments hung about the neck and were used in rapid succession—pan pipes, cornet, mouth organ and so on. At the time I saw him he played a flageolet, accompanying himself with drums and cymbals. Another curiosity is the man of Tower Hill who amuses the lunch-time strollers by extricating himself out of chains and a strait jacket. Begging, pure and simple, seems to have almost disappeared from the London streets, even the most impoverished making an attempt to offer some trifle in exchange for a coin. Mayhew's book on the London poor is one of several books necessary for a study of the city's pavement life, of which now only fragments remain. Victorian London was full of such harrowing sights as the man I saw years ago, legless and armless, selling ballads, or the festering bundles of rags covering the remains of a woman I saw more recently on the Embankment—a bundle of rags, however, that did not lack vocal abilities. On my starting to draw her, she cursed in language which would have given even a bargee the shudders, and so I pushed off.

Of street popular art, the pavement artists must be included here, although they are not among the unknown or little-known aspects of London, but their brightly coloured, oddly naive drawings chalked on the flagstones are always worth seeing. I think perhaps the most attractive ensemble of popular art is Queenie and her owner and cart, who are found in and about St. John's Wood High Street. Queenie is a large, grey, well-tempered bitch, who sits on a covered box with a bowl for pennies in front

Anarchists lived here: Jubilee Street, Whitechapel

Shoreditch bazaar: Fashion Street

of her. She wears a Union Jack waistcoat, well padded, with the words 'Good Luck Queenie' written on it. Her owner, also addicted to popular art, turns the handle of an old gramophone from a little cart, decked out with more Union Jacks, to which in December are added cardboard figures of Father Christmas.

Without doubt, the best way to start a tour of Bermondsey is to approach it by way of the Jamaica Road, plunging into Shad Thames behind Courage's Brewery at Horselydown just beyond Tower Bridge. However, Bermondsey, which contains the one-time village of Rotherhithe, adjoins Southwark, and from Tooley Street runs the old High Street of Bermondsey, Bermondsey Street. This thoroughfare is worth a visit, in particular for the old house I have drawn on p. 89. As can be seen in the drawing, it has an attractive oriel window and overhanging top storey of weatherboarding. This weatherboarded upper storey is very similar to those of the weavers' houses in Fournier Street, Spitalfields. The names of Grange Walk and Crucifix Lane in this area are a reminder of the extensive priory which stood here in the Middle Ages. I have already mentioned the pretty toy Gothic front of the Parish Church in the chapter on London Gothic. Bermondsey Street smells of spice, a characteristic smell met along Shad Thames, but it has its own special odour—the vague drifting smells of tanneries. In the last century, one of the lowliest ways of earning a living, to which only the near destitute had recourse, was the supply of an article called 'Pure' to the tanneries of Bermondsey. 'Pure' was nothing more than dogs' dung gathered in various parts of London by 'Pure-finders'; this choice article of commerce was used in the process of leather dressing, and was supplied to the tanners at a few pence per bucket.

Besides the parish church and the church of St. Mary Rotherhithe (full of interest as a fine early Georgian church of a riverside, boat building village), there is the church of St. James in the Jamaica Road, a Grecian church by Savage, the architect of the Gothic St. Luke's, Chelsea. Savage's Grecian design is as impressive as his Chelsea Gothic; the great space of the interior with its coffered ceiling and Ionic columns is of exceptional quality, but the church is poor and requiring attention in the way of repairs. It dates from 1827 to 1829. Opposite the narrow streets leading to the river by Tower Bridge are more of those barrack-like blocks of nineteenth-century flats, which, like the Peabody blocks, are wonderfully evocative of the period. Devon Mansions on Jamaica Road are typical, but they have recently been painted in modern colour schemes. The iron railings, once a nondescript colour, are now pale blue, and the window-frames also, and pinky grey paint has replaced the whitewash rubbed by years of greasy shoulders on the open stairs.

The drawing of Shad Thames on p. 87 shows you what to expect in this long riverside street—tall warehouses, iron bridges, lowering alley ways and gents' lavatories. These can be enjoyed the whole length of the river from Horselydown to Deptford. The streets bend round the Thames for most of the distance, only turning away from the river at one or two places. The appearance of Shad Thames has changed little during the last century, the only modern innovations being the lorries that now congest the narrow streets in place of horse-drawn wagons. These Thames-side streets, built up on each side with cliff-like, well-used warehouses, smell strongly of spice, and the language heard here can be best described as Anglo-Saxon. Not far from Shad Thames, going east to the point where the Jamaica Road bends at Dockhead, is the site of one of the most notorious of the early nineteenth-century rookeries—Jacob's Island, known to all readers of *Oliver Twist*. This has now been swept away. In its time, it rivalled the rookery of St. Giles, Seven Dials, and Tom-all-Alones in Westminster, as a place of wretchedness and misery. Most of the crazy houses were dropping into the mud, and were built on piles above the ditch, a ditch that served as a supply of drinking water as well as a depository for dead cats and dogs.

Rotherhithe is, I think, the most interesting quarter of Bermondsey. Like most of the area, it has become the scene of much rebuilding in the shape of large blocks of flats, replacing war-damaged property, and as part of a general slum clearance programme. The rebuilding has inevitably caused a severe loss of character and interest. Much of Jamaica Road from Dockhead to the Queen Charlotte is lined with empty property at the time of writing, all of it awaiting demolition. Jamaica Road, by the way, takes its name from an inn called The Jamaica, which stood in Cherry Garden Street; Pepys refers to it in his *Diary*, as well as the Cherry Garden itself. Small one-man businesses flourish here—newsagents, dairies and there are a few old-fashioned drapery stores, ironmongers and fruiterers, and in the area between the Jamaica Road and Grange Road are some hundreds of little streets, most of them lined with trees. In the bay windows of parlours, aspidistras loom large in the opening between the lace curtains. Many of these Bermondsey aspidistras are of advanced age, having been handed down as part of the household gods, and their leaves are kept shiny by the regular application of milk. The way to see Rotherhithe is to follow Paradise Street from the War Memorial opposite the Queen Charlotte and turn into Rotherhithe Street, following it all the way to St. Mary's Church, and then, where the warehouses close in again, carrying on along the street as far as Deptford. Paradise Street had some ancient, battered houses, some-what French in appearance, but the most unusual sight still remaining is the early nineteenth-century police station of London, stock brick and very

The Yiddish Theatre in the Commercial Road

handsome. It was, no doubt, a private residence in the early nineteenth century, and has some good ironwork at the front. Police stations might form a study for those in search of off-beat London. Some of the most interesting are unfortunately disappearing—the century old one at Sydenham, for example, and the forbidding one in Albany Street. It is to be hoped that the huge Victorian Harrow Road Police Station will remain intact.

On the edge of the river in Rotherhithe Street, adjoining the Angel, is a small group of old houses constituting almost the last of those on this part of the river. Although altered, they date from the middle of the eighteenth century, and belonged originally to ships' captains and the like. The two most interesting are The Jolly Waterman, a public house up to the late 1920's, and The Little Midshipman, once my London studio, and later, after I left, the riverside *pied-à-terre* of Mr. Antony Armstrong-Jones, as he was then. The old houses are worth a visit as they may ultimately disappear under one of the rebuilding schemes that have done so much to destroy London. The Little Midshipman, which I christened after the old house in *Dombey and Son*, had its moments of popular glory at the time of Princess Margaret's wedding. When I acquired the house, it had served for many years as the offices of a shipping company. All these houses have curious old rooms, odd staircases and so on, most of all The Little Midshipman— Number 59—which has, in addition to a three-bay window perched over the river, some mid eighteenth-century rooms with pine panelled walls, and as it stands rather higher than the others, was the only house in which the Thames failed to make its way during the floods of January, 1953, when Rotherhithe was awash. From these houses, a walk of a short distance between the warehouses, at this point smelling of flour, brings one to St. Mary's Rotherhithe, already mentioned. The church comes suddenly into view, surrounded by trees, a nice old-fashioned rural effect like an old drawing, and near the church is the pretty school house, with quaint figures of a boy and girl, a building belonging to the middle of the eighteenth century, being built by subscription in 1745. Close by are the old watch and engine houses of the parish.

Of the other off-beat experiences available in Rotherhithe (Redriff, by the way, in the time of Gulliver, one of its famous inhabitants) is the underground station. Here the line runs under the river from Rotherhithe to Wapping, through the Thames Tunnel engineered by Brunel and opened in 1843. The station below ground has a Doré-like appearance and a peculiarly pungent smell of damp. Strange exhalations steal down the walls, and in the narrow trough that runs along the back of the platform at the intersection of the wall, small fish have found a lodging. Even the trains have an unusual quality—steam trains come through on occasion— and, as regards the underground, I have travelled in old carriages still displaying the initials of the Metropolitan Railway in sandblasted glass on the panels of the hand-operated sliding doors.

8

Stucco and Gilt

THE TITLE to this last chapter has been chosen merely to indicate something of the vast range of curiosities, architectural and otherwise, to be found in London. To seek them out is one of the free entertainments offered by London. Only a few of an infinite number can be mentioned here, and such pleasures take all possible forms—cafés, early cinemas, bits of unexpected decoration or enamel advertisements, for example. Things of no artistic value or architectural significance in themselves, often enough, they are simply unconsidered trifles which, by falling into no accepted artistic or historical category, are greatly undervalued. It is certain that such odd and stimulating things survive only fortuitously, in London especially, beset as it is by bureaucrats, property developers who pay little regard to either preserving the subtler qualities of London or the thoughts and feelings of those who may prefer London to be left alone and who are mostly powerless to alter the course of events.

So the time for seeking after the curious and original is now; the London of the future (apart from its historic monuments on whose merits all agree) will be a place of mammoth blocks, of steel and glass hives for the production of paper work or for the accommodation of human ants, a new and ugly Babylon. And there were no aspidistras in Babylon.

Early cinemas of the Edwardian period and up to the Great War occurred in all the London suburbs; these, often family owned, have been less able to stand up to the competition of television than the larger circuits, and consequently many have disappeared or else been modernized and spoiled like the Classic in King's Road, Chelsea. Many of these cinemas were of a delightfully ham-fisted Baroque, with fat Tuscan columns that appeared to be in danger of being squashed by the loads they supported. This exaggerated entasis was equalled by an exaggerated abundant decoration—swags, festoons and the like carried out in stucco or terracotta. I have never

103

been fortunate enough to find a Gothic cinema, though Tudor style ones occurred. Cinemas followed the pattern of shapes evoked by the theatre and were naturally built in the prevailing style of the day, i.e. Edwardian Baroque, redolent of Imperial expansion and big cigars. Fortunately the earliest cinema in London—the earliest in the country, in fact—still survives in Wilton Road, Victoria—the Biograph, originally the Bioscope. My drawing of it is reproduced on page 119. Pimlico people have been 'going to the Bio' since it was built in 1905 by an American, George Washington Grant. The Bio still has its classical façade, and apart from changes in the equipment, the only alteration was when the auditorium was enlarged, the new wall being a replica of the old. But the gas jets have gone and the commissionaires with heavy moustaches—gone like the horse buses that used to run along the Vauxhall Bridge Road. When my drawing was made, the customers were watching 'The Fiend from Outer Space' instead of Mary Pickford as the little slavey with a heart of gold.

Inside, two Corinthian columns (illustrated at the head of this page), wallpapered with Anaglypta below, support the projection box, the width of which is that of the cinema in 1905. Below the 'ceiling' formed by the box runs an Edwardian egg and dart moulding—a typical early cinema decoration. In the foyer is a framed copy of *The Biograph Weekly News*, distributed gratis. This forms rich reading at the present day. The issue in the frame is that for the week commencing September 16th, 1929, and has the headline: 'Talkies Coming Here!!' A letter from the manager announces 'our first talking picture'—'Show Boat' on September 30th. Elsewhere in the paper a newsy item states that 'workmen are labouring day and night to bring you the greater talkies as soon as possible'. Other forthcoming attractions of that period included William Boyd in 'The Cop' and a supporting film called 'The Mystery of the Louvre'. Betty Balfour was to appear in 'Paradise' and Rin Tin Tin in 'The Million Dollar Collar'. Prices were 2s., 1s. 3d. and 9d., children at reduced rates, 'special children's matinee 4d.' (I remember those children's 4d. matinees; how noisy they were and the way the films rained! And those serials, ending each instalment on a fantastic note of drama—the heroine hanging by her finger-tips over a well of crocodiles. The week which had to elapse before her fate could be known was unendurable, but next time she had simply

104

Interior. The St. Gothard Café

got out, one never knew how, and we were building up to a new crisis even more hair-raising than last week's dilemma.)

No doubt those impecunious or thrifty patrons who ricked their necks in the ninepennies would be glad of the optician's advert in the free paper, for an optician was offering 'Good News for the Weak Sighted'—spectacles 'complete with spherical lenses' for 4s. 6d. with sight testing thrown in for nothing—'Usual price 21s.' Generous measures!

If you have a mind for it, you can pretty well drink all round the clock in London pubs, by an elaborate system of timing which includes visiting dockyard pubs with special licensing hours and those of Covent Garden also with special arrangements for the convenience of market men. One of the striking characteristics of London pubs is the way in which different pubs have an appeal to different kinds of patrons. I am not here referring to those the character of which has been deliberately fostered by the brewers by shipping in odds and ends, as these, of course, are purely artificial; I mean the genuine ones where people of a like turn of mind tend to gravitate, much in the way that the eighteenth-century coffee houses tended to attract clients with interests in common. There is the Coach and Eight in Upper Richmond Road, by Putney Bridge, for instance—full of Spy cartoons, old maps, prints and rowing relics, as far as I know London's only rowing pub. There are legal pubs—the one now called the Magpie and Stump behind the Law Courts is an example, and there are others on the fringes of the Inner and Middle Temples. In Dean Street, Soho, the Frenchmen congregate at the York Minster, and there is the wonderfully named Essex Serpent for Covent Garden, the Opera Tavern (both these have fine florid Victorian exteriors) for those 'of Drury Lane' and another splendidly named pub, the Steam Packet, for the men of Billingsgate. City hostelries for City gents are many, including historical ones like the George and Vulture, Mr. Pickwick's refuge, and the Jamaica Wine House. There are intellectuals' pubs in Hampstead, where advanced thinkers constellate, artists' pubs in Chelsea, some lined with paintings for sale, pubs for journalists, of course, and wine bars, including the wonderfully period interior of El Vino's in Fleet Street (iron tables, lincrusta wallpaper and a magnificent period telephone, all quite unspoilt), pubs for cricket enthusiasts, homosexuals' pubs, even, where queers meet queers, and one patronized by Lesbians.

London pubs are rich in all the trappings of the Victorian age, which knew exactly how a town pub should appear. A fine one is illustrated here —The King and Queen in the Harrow Road. This is nineteenth-century Baroque at its most florid. Grey marble columns rise from a mosaic floor, raised a step above the pavement. There is splendid ironwork—iron letters and wrought iron—over the door. The words 'Saloon Bar' have a bucolic

Pharmacy in Gloucester Road, S.W.7

abandon, showing the influence of *art nouveau*. (I have included in this chapter the best *art nouveau* pub in London—the Black Friar, near *The Times* office.) These highly ornamented pubs of the 1860–90 period show

107

great skill in stone cutting and wood carving. For those who take pleasure in the intersection of planes, there is much to admire in the way variously intricate surfaces, diverse mouldings and arabesques run into and fuse with each other. Such architecture is the antithesis of modern movements. The architects of the late Victorian pubs and music-halls knew exactly what the situation demanded—extravagance, exuberance and plenty of decoration for its own sake. Fortunately, there is no theory of design behind such buildings: the architects helped themselves to what they wanted like Kipling's Homer. The result is exactly right. The King and Queen has much mahogany and engraved and embossed glass. These in combination are basic to the Victorian pub. So, too, are the highly polished mirrors, deeply bevelled, that are the support for highly wrought paintings. These belong to the 1880's usually, the subjects generally being of bulrushes over which swallows are on the wing, perhaps with kingfishers or other birds of the wayside stream or country brook, corn, barley and the like. Such designs are also carried out in painted glass—leaded lights as they are called in the trade. With them go the pictures in tile, usually found by the door to the saloon or private bar or lining the wall of the saloon bar corridor. Tiled pictures belong to the period when the work of Walter Crane was at its most popular—they resemble his style closely, together with that of Albert Moore and a suggestion of the Grosvenor Gallery.

The Lamb, Leadenhall Market, on page 113, has windows with sprays of corn, as well as fine pub lamps. Birds and foliage also occur on those small movable screens so arranged as to give the patrons of the saloon bar a privacy denied to those frequenting the public bar—a characteristic Victorian contrivance and one found in many London pubs to this day. In all these pubs, the fittings—the Brewers' advertisements in engraved and etched plate glass, the beer-pulls of porcelain delightfully decorated with roses, gold rings or the willow pattern, the elaborate central wagon or island that served all the bars, including the jug and bottle, even the gas or electric light fittings—were designed to create a compelling, lavish atmosphere. Fine examples of embossed and etched glass sometimes in combination with back painting occur all over London, but perhaps the finest are those in the Red Lion, St. James's, a pub full of panels in embossed mirror glass. Gas lights were placed in the main pub windows, two or three to each window, stemming from a highly polished brass bar. At first open fish-tail burners were used; later highly decorated globes replaced the gas flares. These fitments can still be found in London, occasionally, if still in use, converted to electric light.

The bar counter and its imposing fittings is invariably the *pièce de resistance* of the London pub. Mostly horseshoe shaped on plan, the island

Purdey's, Mayfair

Queen Anne's Gate Restaurant

rises in an infinite number of curly brackets, railed shelves with turned balustrades, brilliant mirrors and bottles (the display of bottles is a later innovation—during the nineteenth century spirits were kept in barrel-shaped porcelain containers)—the whole rising up like a great organ, often surmounted by a clock under an elaborately broken pediment. Ferns and aspidistras flourish on these counters. These items of decoration are still favoured, especially in the East End, together with plastic surfaced advertisements, little pots of that abominable dyed weed dredged up near Southend and royal portraits. Although, as I have said, the East End is losing some of its strongly focal character, the old life of the pubs in those parts of London still persists. A week-end pub crawl in such places as Shoreditch, Stepney and Hackney is the way to see it at first hand. Here the East End 'ma' continues to flourish, the large sized, perhaps even pneumatic specimen who was no stranger to Phil May and Albert Chevalier, joins in the chorus, supported at the rear by a buttoned horsehair seat and at the front by a large Guinness. Such period characters must disappear sometime—that is where the funeral parlour comes in; if so, however, they are at once replaced by replicas, presumably on a system known only to the East End.

One of the finest and least-known London pubs is the Crown, Cunningham Place, on the edge of St. John's Wood and mistressy Maida Vale. The Crown is magnificently Late Victorian, full of old wallpaper and marble, and possessing a billiard room complete in every detail, down to the horsehair seats. Go there in a straw boater in summertime; smoke a Woodbine, and think about Kitchener.

The nineteenth-century London pub described above was preceded by the gin palace, the chief feature of which was the large room and long horizontal bar. Gin palaces have quite disappeared, but Henekey's in Holborn ought to be visited as the nearest resemblance. This is a most interesting place. One side of the vast room is taken up by a gallery with barrels of colossal size; below this is the back of the bar with an assortment of smaller barrels, kegs and bottles and in front of this is the bar counter. On the opposite side is a set of little boxes like Victorian lifts. These are snuggeries for private parties, an admirable arrangement. Most picturesque of all is the cast iron stove, a mysterious affair without visible pipes. This is a choice piece of Victoriana and still in use, apparently consuming its own smoke. There must be other stoves like this in London but the only one in my recollection is that at Hoare's Bank and no longer in use.

From pubs the London cafés and restaurants are a natural transition; I mean, of course, those lesser-known ones possessing a marked period flavour. Such places as Rules in Maiden Lane, notwithstanding its rich late nineteenth-century interior, are therefore outside my theme; so for

III

this reason are the Grill Room of the Café Royal, the Criterion Restaurant, where Toulouse-Lautrec had his porterhouse steaks, and one or two others. However, I cannot resist mentioning the Hamilton Hall in the Great Eastern Hotel, near Liverpool Street. The Hamilton Hall is part of the Abercorn Rooms, and is named after the chairman of the railway at the turn of the century, Lord Claud Hamilton. The whole room is full of mirrors and marble, allegorical figures and paintings, and was in fact copied from The Palais Soubise in Paris. It is remarkable that, though the décor is eighteenth-century French, the effect is unmistakably Edwardian. It dates from 1901, and I recommend a visit, seeing also at the same time the fantastic Victorian Elizabethan bar of the hotel, which is so evocative that one gets the sensation of having stepped into a picture by Stacey Marks.

Many small cafés and restaurants still remain with a pronounced period flavour, but they are a vanishing race. One of the best is the Court Tea Room (Gentlemen Only) downstairs from a little court near Leadenhall Market. The very name 'tea room' is reminiscent of *art nouveau*. The Court Tea Room is a very complete study in Edwardian comfort and décor. The chairs here are what might be called 'early Heal' or 'early Maple', and have green leather seats studded with nails. The tables, tiled in dark green, are splendid—dark oak and ornamented with a little twisty bit of *art nouveau*; a ledge underneath holds copies of *Punch* and *Country Life*. In fact, the whole place has a pronounced club-like atmosphere. Hat stands blossom upwards in shapes resembling honeysuckle flowers, and the walls are lined with mirrors over which droop bell-shaped electric light shades. The cornice above the mirrors is decorated with blue and white plates (Walter Crane school once more). A Victorian fireplace with overmantel is in complete accord with the rest. Marble and tiled fireplaces were a feature of Victorian cafés. Another occurs in one of the best remaining small restaurants, the St. Gothard Café in Fulham Road. Even the entrance door here is exactly right, being delicately patterned with scrolls and leafage sandblasted on the plate glass, with the owner's name and a pretty little Swiss motif in the centre. Adjoining the door is the café counter, backed by a high wooden fixture with shelves and brackets, rather like the behind-the-bar fitment in the pubs just discussed. But here, instead of bottles, is an assortment of chocolate, sweets and tobacco. Crimson plush seats, seen in my drawing on page 105, are a feature of this nice old café, and marble tables. Note the partitions with little glass panels, ornamented with the word 'Bovril' in a border of Greek honeysuckle ornament, and the little shelves above, railed off by tiny turned columns, and, of course, the vases and aspidistra pots. Most proprietors of such cafés unload such old-fashioned features, and move in with plastic and chromium horrors, nowadays, resulting in an utter loss

The Lamb Tavern, Leadenhall Market

of character and interest; it is rare to find one so complete, even to the gas lights.

In a pure *art nouveau* style and all but complete is the Kardomah in Market Lane, Eastcheap. Going down the stairs, you feel like an old issue of the *Studio*. The stairs themselves have dark brown verticals of wood—a design of Voysey—filled in with lozenge glass of red, yellow and green. From it, one can survey the mosaic-lined café, an interior that is completely *art nouveau*: only the counter and the people are wrong. A blue iris pattern appears on the wall, and above the shelf-like dado, at intervals along the frieze, are huge surprising bosses of burnished copper with green centres, like Viking shields. The tables are Art and Craft productions, the umbrella stand also, a vintage production pierced with heart-shaped holes. These and the sham-timbered roof give the place a baronial air, an effect aided by a Gothic door. There is a strange contrast between the formalized sagging shapes of the *art nouveau* patterns and the baronial flavour, the latter seeming to call for rushes, various hairy dogs and an odd minstrel or two, and the former for men with waxed moustaches and celluloid collars.

Art nouveau still maintains a foothold in Germany, France and Holland in such things as shop fronts, ironwork and lettering. In England where, surprisingly, it all started (though the origins of *art nouveau* are too complex to be discussed here), it faded long ago—killed by the jazz age, except for odd survivals such as the leaded lights in the windows of suburban semi's, where it shows extraordinary persistence. London is not too well off for *art nouveau* on a large scale, the best example being the tiled and mosaic meat and poultry hall at Harrods. Another bit of *art nouveau* is illustrated on page 116, this being the Black Friar pub I have previously mentioned. Conventionalized carvings of monks support the door canopies, and there is a profusion of mosaic and beaten metalwork. Art nouveau is a movement deserving more extended study than it has as yet received: the stiff formality of its shapes, blended with sagging unbeauteous curves are an outward expression of the *fin de siècle*, pulled this way and that, just as the harsh forms of today, destined to be equally outdated, are a sufficient indication of the madness of the mid twentieth century. The Black Friar is Victorian above and *art nouveau* below. The door I have drawn is of white stone and marble with an infilling of coloured mosaic; the metal plates by the doors, 'To the Saloon' and 'Worthington Ales on draught', have figures of monks, and the interior is as rich as the exterior.

Yet another of these pleasant old-fashioned cafés is illustrated on page 110, The Queen Anne's Gate Restaurant. This has a very period feature in the shape of porcelain letters on the windows, offering afternoon teas. This form of signwriting, fixed on the glass by means of cement, occurs also in

The King and Queen in the Harrow Road

Ars Nouveau
Blackfriars —
The Blackfriar
Doorway

pubs and on the windows of the older type of chocolate and sweet shops, advertising Cadbury's or Fry's chocolate, with the royal coat of arms, a relic of the days of knickerbockers, Norfolk jackets and Eton collars. The Queen Anne's Gate Restaurant has a late Victorian or Edwardian flavour. There is a large canopy, rather like the top of a sideboard, now painted pale blue. The dark stained finish of a previous generation shows through the paint. The walls are tiled, inset with mirrors—those mirrors that reflect each other down long corridors. These walls are bordered with blue and white, also yellow and grey tiles, and there is a deep tiled cornice of blue fruits and leaves on white. Fine engraved panels are a feature of the café, some of them can be seen in my drawing, and form a piquant foil to the sauce bottles and adverts for '7-up'. With these old-fashioned restaurants might be grouped the dining-rooms and, on a higher plane, the Victorian oyster rooms. Of these, the two best, I think—speaking artistically, of course— are Gow's 'Oyster and Shellfish Warehouse' in Old Broad Street, which has a fascia of probably the finest Victorian lettering in the City, and Sweeting's Oyster Rooms.

Woburn Walk with its double row of shops has already been mentioned in passing, and is, in any case, justly appreciated. But London has many other shops less well known, and many of these possess character and interest in various degrees. Pharmacies occupy a prominent place, both from their number and quality. Many of the best are almost unknown examples, for instance, the early nineteenth-century one in Richmond Terrace, Islington, which has Corinthian columns and Gothic arched windows—a hybrid. There is one in Wimbledon dating from a couple of decades later in 1840 Tudor-Elizabethan; this is of much interest as it possesses the original fittings including the little wooden drawers for drugs. Belgravia is a good area for pharmacies; among the best is Gulliver's, off Eaton Square, once again with period fittings—a cut-glass door handle, in particular. In the great periods, such small things were not considered too insignificant to receive artistic treatment, and were, in fact, carefully thought out in order to contribute to a harmonious scheme. To develop a discerning eye for such minutiae is an essential step if one is to benefit from the prophylactic qualities of architecture. I have drawn a much later pharmacy on p. 107, and I proposed to discuss it in connexion with another drawing, that on p. 109 of Purdey's, the gunsmiths in Mayfair. Both these two shops belong to a rather special kind of Victorian architecture of the late 1870's and especially the 1880's, which has received little attention and has no precise label. You might, for want of a better name, call it Early Oscar Wilde though this lacks definition. In both, a kind of Gothicy flavour (the iron work above Purdey's façade and the doors and corbel in Cooper's pharmacy) is combined with debased Renaissance details. Fused together, these styles combine to form this pure late Victorian style which is found in various parts of London. Ornamental pilasters are a feature, together with exaggerated curved pediments, cut brick and the sunflower device. This architecture coincides with the fashionable acceptance of the work of Morris and Co., the nursery illustrations, formal and classically flavoured, of Crane and his followers, and the beginning of the Art and Craft movement, of which Norman Shaw's suburb of Bedford Park is a monument—a memorial to the fortunately faded dream world of *News from Nowhere*— a fusty, unattractive Socialist utopia peopled by handloom weavers, cheerful and vastly disagreeable, at work on folksy objects.

The style shown in my two drawings is, however, a quite separate development—contemporaneous but, I think, unconnected. Only the Victorians could produce it. It is quite handsome in a stolid kind of way and has the air of solidity found in nineteenth-century banks and Pall Mall clubs. This late-flowing, brackish Rennaissance stream soon dried up; the style had quite gone by the 1890's, being overtaken in popularity by *art nouveau*. The two lamps outside Cooper's are rather fine, and Purdy's, a wonderfully preserved period establishment with gas brackets, has a magnificent Victorian room, ornamented with old photographs and sporting equipment. The shop still retains an early telephone, a wall instrument, of impressive appearance. There are few shops in London so carefully cherished.

Brompton Road has at least two shops of interest—Burkett's, the Poulterers, and T. Debry Fils. Burkett's has a tiled interior with a deep frieze of acanthus pattern raised in pale cream against a background of blue-green. Lock's hat shop in St. James's Street is too well known to be included here, but it reminds me that they wear straw boaters at Burkett's, which is exactly the right headgear for a butcher, poulterer or fishmonger. Debry Fils is somewhat modernized, but the Edwardian white-painted window remains, and the period atmosphere, too, no doubt because of the mirrors still in place in the alcove and also the large be-ribboned boxes of chocolates ranged behind the counter. This mention of chocolates brings me to that delightful shop, Prestat's, in South Moulton Street. The interior is full of mirrors and gilding and mahogany showcases full of chocolate boxes, and there is an old-fashioned pair of scales. There are those tall cylindrical glass jars with big pointed stoppers, full of sugared almonds and chocolate dragees. The mirrors reflect each other and the sweet jars doubling one's pleasure. Only a hansom or a Victoria waiting outside is wanting or the exquisite, civilized, late nineteenth-century atmosphere would be complete in all details. Only Floris, the perfumiers, in Jermyn Street, is so fine, and the latter has the added attraction of shell pink electric

Saturday afternoon at the Biograph, Victoria

light shades of Edwardian vintage. To close this short list (which is only a sample of the considerable number to be found and appreciated), there is one of quite a different type, Hopkin Purvis, the oil and colourmen in Greek Street, Soho. This has a sober, mid-Victorian Classical façade and an old-fashioned crane folded against the windows. The interior is also good; here again occur the rows of little wooden drawers formerly found in pharmacies, colourmen and seed shops.

Another special variety of London shops is the Welsh dairy. Dairying in one of the large cities—London, for preference—was one of the occupations to which the Welsh naturally turned in the general exodus from their homeland. They made money in other ways, of course, but dairying in London was generally favoured. There must be dozens of little London dairies with the name of Jones on the fascia. The Welsh, like the Jews, are gregarious, and could hope to find family friends already in the trade, but today the big combines have created a situation in which there is no longer the same scope for the small private dairy, perhaps with only a single roundsman. Many of the Welsh dairies have little Staffordshire groups in the window, or sometimes a large pottery churn, gold-banded with a lithographed picture of a farm on the side towards the window. I think perhaps my favourite apart from the blue-tiled Evan's dairy in Warren Street is the Park Farm Dairy in Tachbrook Street. Outside are brown and yellow patterned tiles and inside the inevitable mirrors, a marble counter and a showcase ornamented with tiles. These tiles are rather fine, the subjects, transfer printed in black on cream, being of deer and other animal subjects and Victorian cottage door and village scenes, oddly in contrast with the pallid surrounding streets.

It is often impossible to guess at what lies behind the modernized façades of London shops. In many cases, the exterior is misleading and merely masks the old building behind. Two instances might be mentioned here— Dollond and Aitchison in the Strand and one in Oxford Street I accidentally discovered in novel circumstances. This occurred while I was at the Slade, and in search of a picture frame, I was recommended to an old Jew who sat with a few frames on the pavement of Rathbone Place, in front of some bomb-damaged property. Legend had it that students used to sell him the drawings done as corrections by Tonks or Schwabe at a shilling each in the pre-war years. However, the old fellow, who looked like a Rembrandt drawing, asked me to meet him one night about seven. He led the way across Oxford Street, unlocked the plate glass door of one of the inexpensive dress shops, full of palais de danse-type outfits, and led me downstairs. The room below was empty, but for the top of a magnificent staircase, elaborately ornamented, which ran into yet another lower floor. It was one of the finest

Drawing-room at the Cavendish

staircases I have seen in central London, and dated from the early eighteenth century. The room in which we landed, well below the pavement level, had a cornice of similar rich quality. Moreover, it was crammed with eighteenth- and nineteenth-century drawings and watercolours, mostly unframed and collecting dust; there were drawings everywhere in that room of mystery, in great heaps and piled high on a large central table. I often wonder what became of the drawings, the Jew and the balustraded staircase, so richly carved. . . .

Before long, the Cavendish Hotel in Jermyn Street will have disappeared, and I am glad to place a bit of it on record in this book—the two drawings in this chapter being of reflections in one of the rococo mirrors of the drawing room and one of the wonderful marble washhand basins, complete with brass soap trays, of the Edwardian period. The Cavendish is the last London hotel to possess the old-fashioned country hotel atmosphere. In fact, the noise of London fails to penetrate into the mellow recesses of the Cavendish, and even in the hotel garden, the song of the birds—thrushes and blackbirds mainly—is louder than the sound of the traffic. The private room where Rosa Lewis received special friends remains exactly as she left it, a place of old photographs, paintings and chintz-covered chairs. These wonderful chintz settees and chairs are a feature of the Cavendish, and make it the right place to recover from overmuch tramping of London pavements. Parts of the Cavendish are quite old, but most of it is early nineteenth century with an Edwardian flavour added. This is seen in the big dining-room, where the chairs are a mixture of Chippendale style and 'early Heal'; the same atmosphere of solid comfort is found in the drawing-room, furnished with occasional tables, plenty of the chintz-covered settees, oriental carpets and paintings, including a small Sickert of the races at Dieppe.

It is sad to think of the Cavendish disappearing, no doubt to be replaced by some Grand Babylon Hotel, but it will at least have retained its special quality to the last. An up-to-date proprietor would have introduced a King Edward VII bar (a nasty affair carried out by a fashionable decorator) or a Lily Langtry room long ago to catch the tourist trade. And I wonder what will happen to the little memorial stone which Rosa Lewis placed by the marble steps 'in loving memory of Kippy', her little dog who made these steps his vantage point for so many years?

The Cavendish is only one of the many aspects of London which are vanishing at an accelerating speed. Most of the things in this book are destined to go the same way in a London that has become the prey of bureaucrats, developers and destroyers; today the whip, tomorrow the

Edwardian opulence; bathroom fittings at the Cavendish

scorpion. Off-beat London is hopelessly out of date, and it simply does not pay. I hope, therefore, this book will be a stimulus to explore the under-valued parts of London before it is too late, before it vanishes as if it had never been. The old London was essentially a domestic city—never a grandiose or bombastic one. Its architecture was therefore scaled to human proportions. Of the new London, the London of take-over bids and soul-destroying office blocks, the least said, the better.